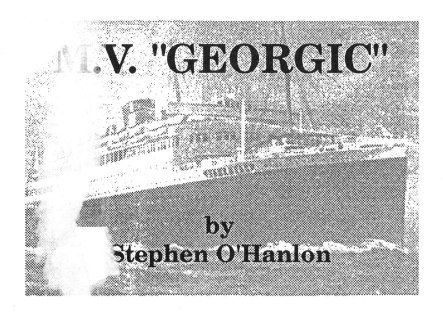

M.V. "GEORGIC"

by
Stephen O'Hanlon

First published 1996 by Countyvise Limited, 1 & 3 Grove Road,
Rock Ferry, Birkenhead, Wirral, Merseyside L42 3XS
Copyright © Stephen O'Hanlon

Set in 11pt New Century Schoolbook

Printed by Birkenhead Press Limited, 1 & 3 Grove Road,
Rock Ferry, Birkenhead, Wirral, Merseyside L42 3XS

ISBN 0 907768 95 4

This book is dedicated to my dear mother, Lill.

*Also my father Steve (deceased) a Seaman and
my stepfather Arthur, (deceased) an ex Sergeant Major.*

ACKNOWLEDGEMENTS

I wish to thank all who have helped in the compiling of this book, including my dear wife Bridget, my daughter, daughters in law, my two sons, my sister Elizabeth, my niece, my brother Tom and his wife, Sheila, and my brothers Jim and Terry.

Also, my brother James O'Hanlon, who is the artist who painted the front cover and produced the sketches within the text.

Also the following in Australia:

G.R. and M. Elliot, Robert Southey, Graham Harrison, Jean Gould, Bob McKenzea, George Parker, Mrs E. O'Shea, David Wilcox, Mrs D. Woodward, J.E. Holmes, Mrs V.M. Hicks, Miss J. Nash, C.E. Eldridge, R.N., Yvonne Melzer, Teresa Dean, K.A. Punter, D. Cross, Kathleen Barrard, Mary C. Rhind, George Madderly, Bert Love, J.W. Ellis, M.D. Stephenson, Dilys Clark, A.J. West, G.G. Jermy, and Mary A. Tomlin

And: The Admiralty M.O.D.: The Weekly Times, Australia: Western Australia Newspapers: Herald-Sun Newspapers, Melbourne: Mr W. Anderson, Shipping Grades, Liverpool: Janet (M.R.T. typist): Vickey Caulter (typist): Ken Hale, Jim Duggan, Tom Lally, Liverpool University (Andrea Owens): Cunard Archives: Liverpool Maritime Museum Archives: Sir Edward Heath: The High Commission of the Commonweath of Australia and the Liverpool Retired Seafarers.

Stephen O'Hanlon

John Allen

The name was big John Allen
A seaman from the past
Who loved to talk of Ireland
And his days before the mast.

He sailed on ships the seven seas
From Australia to Hong Kong
Then home through gales and round the Cape
To the Oak Tree for a song.

On a road that leads to Prescot
And past a village mill
Then on to Little Whiston
And his Cottage on the Hill.

Peter King, April 1991

INDEX

M. V. Georgic

by
Stephen O'Hanlon

A few short stories have been written about the *M. V. Georgic*. I decided to write a more detailed version including the part, the ship was used for as a troop ship and the emigration run to Australia, Canada and the United States. Not a great deal was to be found in the archives and museums so I decided to try and locate the people who had sailed in her. This I am sure you will appreciate took many months; then consider the ages of the people. However, with the help of many, a list of which you will find in my book, I started writing.

From the time of the launching of *M.V. Georgic* up until 1939 she was first and foremost a luxury liner sailing between the U.K and U.S.A. If she was not doing this, she was world cruising. Regarded as the fastest motor vessel in the world the *Georgic*, her sister ship *Britannic* and many more liners became part of the war effort and so this is where I decided to begin the story of this most loved ship, which seemed to be ridiculed all her life but always did whatever was asked of her. The *M.V. Georgic* made her Maiden Voyage on 25 June 1932 to New York. She carried cabin class passengers only, Off-season fare being £31.15s. (£31.75p.). High season £33.5s. (£33.25p.) 7 days in New York £8.10s. (£8.50p.) 25 days across U.S.A. £61.10s. (£61.50p.)

1

It took 2,000 men 2 years to build. During the war she carried 125,937 service personnel and covered 147,262 miles up to December 1945. She used 40 tons fuel oil per day and averaged 280 miles.

By 1939 she carried three class of passengers fares as follows:-

Cabin Class	£39.10s, Liverpool or Southampton — New York	
Tourist	£27. 10s	" " "
Third	£18.10s	" " "

To this day she holds the record for the longest tow of a ship, 2775 miles.

Between 1945 to 1948 she mostly sailed between Liverpool and Bombay. In 1939 Jack G. Holmes of Melbourne sailed on the *Georgic* on a world cruise. He recalls 'My father shouted me a trip around the world as my 21st Birthday present. On checking my diary I find that we boarded the *Georgic* on 19 August 1939 at Southampton and left for New York at 12 o'clock that day. The *Georgic* was a very fine ship with luxurious cabins, a very good gymnasium and swimming pool and good sports decks, night entertainment including horse racing and housie-housie, which I remember quite well as on one occasion I won $50 which was a fair amount in those days. Also there was a good dance orchestra and of course you could go to the "Talkies."

The Dining Room was very good, the menus in both English and French were most mouthwatering and very comprehensive; in those days Cunard White Star certainly knew how to attract customers. We had the most memorable trip on a most luxurious ship.

During the war the army unit to which I belonged was recalled from the Middle East to defend Australia in 1942, (we were really on our way to Malaya but luckily diverted to Australia). We were camped at Suez before ship boarding. We boarded the *Andes*, a luxurious ship built for the South American trade, but was never used except as a troop ship. As we left Port Tufik there was the dear old *Georgic* with her funnels showing above the water line and a mast showing. Edward Heath, M.P., former Prime Minister wrote in his fascinating book "Edward Heath Travels" — 'I celebrated New Year at a Ball in Cleveland (Ohio) with another Oxford friend, Frank Taplin, who had been noted at Queens for his witty topical lyrics which he sang to his own accompaniment. Gene Krupa's Band, then at the top of its form, whipped up the dances into a frenzy at the Ball and made the evening a wild success. In the next few days I saw a lot of Cleveland, and came to like it very much; shortly afterwards I left for New York and sailed for home on the *Georgic*. It was a gloomy voyage. There were fewer than fifty people on board, and we had to provide our own entertainment. The thought of a submarine attack was never far from our minds. At times the liner seemed to be steaming well off course and she took far longer than normal to complete the voyage. On a dismal Sunday morning in the middle of January we steamed up the Mersey into Liverpool Docks. I was back in Wartime Britain.'

Coincidentally two brothers and myself booked into the Dorset Hotel, New York in 1993. When shown to our bedroom I enquired of the porter why there were so many locks on the door. He informed me that Edward Heath used the suite when in New York and so for security reasons these locks were necessary. He also advised myself and the brothers that whoever used the orthopaedic bed, to be sure to look after it as it belonged to Mr. Heath. I used the bed as I also suffer from back trouble. On the 13th April 1940 the Cunard White Star Company were informed that it was necessary in the national interest, their motor vessel *Georgic* then operating under the Liner Requisition

Scheme should be transferred to non-commercial service. Her great size, 27,759 tons, and her speed of 18 knots admirably adapted her for trooping, as her sister ship the *Britannic* had already successfully shown. When requisitioned the *Georgic* was homeward bound from New York to Liverpool with passengers and a large cargo of foodstuffs and other vital necessities. She docked at Liverpool on April 14th and then with all imaginable speed her cargo was discharged and the passengers' accommodation prepared for her military voyages.

This work was completed by the 20th and on that day the ship left the Mersey under orders for Gourock where she arrived in due course on the following day. And there she lay at anchor until May 24th. The only explanation of such enforced idleness would appear to be that the responsible authorities were in a quandary as to how the vessel might most effectually be employed and were hesitant in arriving at a definite decision. Needless to say such inactivity, especially at a time when every ton of British shipping was urgently required for the service of the nation, was altogether at variance with the traditional policy of her owners, and it was generally realised that the ship might have made a voyage to New York and back during the time she was lying at anchor in the Firth of Clyde.

Between 18th August 1940 she had made six consecutive such round voyages and she had ample time to make another before actually commencing her trooping work. This was not the only idle period of the *Georgic* while under requisition, for after landing evacuees from St.Nazaire on June 18th she did not commence her next voyage, which was to Iceland, until July 25th.

From May 27th to June 18th the *Georgic* was busily employed. On the former date she left Liverpool for Greenock and sailed from the Clyde on the following day, her destination being Andersfjourd, where on June 4th she

4

embarked British troops who had been on service in Norway. On the 6th she shipped further contingents at Narvic and then returned to Greenock where she arrived on June 10th and left on the 13th for Brest and St.Nazaire, and the passengers she took on board there she landed at Liverpool on June 13th.

With regard to the Norwegian expedition the Officer commanding the British troops on board was so well pleased with the ship and her staff that he wrote to the Company on June 10th as follows:- "I should like to bring to your notice the manner in which all departments of this ship have carried out their duties during the past week while evacuating troops from Norway. Every member of the crew from the Commander down has done everything possible for our comfort. The catering has been excellent and notwithstanding the very difficult conditions, the Purser's and Stewards' departments have functioned with extreme smoothness. The outstanding impression has been the extreme courtesy and desire to help shown by all. I shall look forward to again sailing on the *Georgic* in happier times."

On the completion of her Iceland trooping voyage (July 25th to August 6th, 1940) the ship was ordered to Halifax, there to embark Canadian soldiery. On the outward run to that port from Gourock she carried 155 first, 217 second and 864 third class passengers and arrived at Halifax on August 19th. According to the Commanding Officer the conditions under which they travelled did not in any way suggest that the ship was a trooper engaged on war service. To quote his words — "the entire voyage was a fine success. The children were kept busy with their school classes, concerts and games. The grown-ups were generally happy. Food was of fine quality and abundant and much credit is due to the Captain and all other officers for their kindness."

The *Georgic* left Halifax on August 27th 1940 with

a total company on board of 2962 including 152 passengers who were awaiting transport to the United Kingdom. The importance of the food question for such a large personnel had been duly recognised and the Company had cabled to Montreal as to supplementary edible stores required for the homeward run. These were as follows: Lump sugar, dried apricots, dried apples, tomatoes, parsnips — 1000-lbs of each; currants and prunes 500-lbs; 400 boxes of dessert apples and ditto of oranges, together with 100 boxes of grapefruit and half that quantity of lemons. Of butter 5000-lbs was to be supplied and of cheese 2000-lbs. The meat stuffs included 20,000-lbs of loins and ribs of fresh beef, 5000-lbs corned briskets and 2000-lbs of ox-tails, 3000-lbs corned legs of pork, 1200 of corned tongues, 3000-lbs of veal, 1000 roasting chickens and 2000 fowl, 500 pigeons and a like number of turkeys, together with 20,000-lbs of fresh fish.

The vegetable supply was on an equally generous scale for it included 80,000-lbs potatoes, turnips 9000, carrots 8000, cabbage 6000, cauliflowers 4000, onions 3000, beetroot 2000 and beans 500, along with 2400 fresh lettuces, while another item on the list was 100,000 fresh eggs. With such a generous and varied food supply the experts of the *Georgic's* catering department had no difficulty in winning the warm admiration of the Canadian Officers and rank and file she carried, as also did the culinary staffs of the other Cunard White Star liners engaged on trooping service.

Whilst on trooping service she called in at New York in February 1941 after a ten months absence. Members of her crew told their many friends in that port that she had a charmed life. She had been at Narvik, at Brest, and St.Nazaire, a prominent target for Nazi bombers but as one of her company said "They couldn't 'it 'er". They tried enough! This was luck which could not last. Five months later as the *Georgic* lay at Suez a lone German bomber dodging searchlights and anti-aircraft fire, dropped two bombs, both of which hit her leaving her a twisted and burned-out hulk on the beach.

M.V.Georgic 1942 under attack — Suez

To walk round the former Cunard White Star liner *Georgic* today, it is difficult to realise that little over four years ago this famous vessel, bombed and gutted by fire, lay ashore and half submerged in Suez Roads to all intents and purposes a total loss. The story of her subsequent salvaging, of the hazardous long tow from Suez to Port Sudan and thence to Karachi, of the emergency repair work carried out in Karachi and Bombay which culminated in her triumphant voyage home, unescorted, at an average speed of 16 knots and carrying 5,000 tons of cargo, has already been told. Today the *Georgic* is a vastly different ship from the battle scarred vessel which made such a dramatic return to Liverpool in March 1943. Even the exterior appearance of the ship has changed. The two masts and twin stocky funnels which in pre-war years were familiar to all seafarers on the North Atlantic have gone, their place taken by one short foremast and a single funnel. But it is in the interior accommodation that the greatest changes have taken place. No longer is the *Georgic* a great North Atlantic Liner temporarily adapted for the carriage of troops. Today she is first and last a troopship.

7

The whole of the war-time experience in the transportation of millions of service men have gone towards her making. When in March 1943, shortly after her return, it was decided that the *Georgic* should be reconstructed as a troopship, the Sea Transport Division of the Ministry of War Transport were determined that the new ship should strike a new note in trooping. To this end, in conjunction with the Sea Transport Division, sets of plans incorporating new ideas were drawn up by technical experts from the Cunard White Star Company, acting as managers on behalf of the Ministry of War Transport, and Harland & Wolff, of Belfast, to whom, as builders of the original ship, the enormous task of reconstruction had been entrusted. When completed, these blue prints were discussed from every possible angle. Particular attention was paid to the ideal position for recreation rooms and dining facilities; the position and number of canteens required; the type of beds which were likely to prove most popular; the all important questions of ventilation and toilet facilities. A tour of the *'Georgic* then revealed the striking way in which those blue print ideas had become practical realities. They include:

> Recreation rooms and cinema
> Spacious troop mess halls
> Up-to-date and perfectly equipped
>   sleeping quarters
> Elaborate systems of ventilation and
>   broadcasting
> Troop barber's shop
> Shower baths

The promenade deck which in former years housed the main public rooms for cabin passengers has been reconstructed and is now entirely devoted to recreation facilities for troops. The officers' lounge now occupies the site of the former main lounge, the old card room has been assigned to warrant officers, whilst a cinema 'and recreation for troops have been constructed in the spaces which were formerly the cabin smoking room and the long gallery. All these rooms have been simply yet comfortably decorated and furnished with chairs, settees and small tables, including writing tables for letters home.

Another upper deck which ·during the *Georgic's* North Atlantic days was used for bedroom accommodation has been entirely reconstructed and re-designed. Today the portside of this deck is occupied by a series of troop mess halls, fitted with long tables and forms to seat approximately twenty men and equipped with hot and cold service presses. These mess halls are unusually spacious, well lit and ventilated.

Two new and perfectly equipped kitchens have been constructed, one at each end of the halls whilst opposite each mess, large dish-washing facilities and tray racks have been erected. An additional troop mess has been installed on 'C' Deck. On this same deck are to be found the dining room for warrant officers whilst, on the site of the old cabin restaurant, the officers' mess has been constructed.

Meals are prepared and served from the adjoining and original vast kitchen spaces, which have been completely re-equipped and refitted. New standards have been set up in the sleeping accommodation provided for all ranks. The officers have been accommodated on 'A' Deck whilst for other ranks the *Georgic* has been divided into scores of sections in the equipping of which every effort has been made towards greater comfort.

Berths are of the 'standee' type which is popular amongst troops not only because of the sleeping comfort it provides but also because it can be folded up quickly and easily, thus giving more deck room. Adjoining each set of berths, racks for stowing kit and personal gear, scores of coat hooks and small mirrors have been installed. Washing facilities are on an adjoining deck — a special feature being the increased number of shower baths.

An outstanding feature of the new *Georgic* is the new system of ventilation which extends throughout the ship and which has meant an increase of nearly 100 per cent in the number of fans installed. Nowhere is this increase more noticeable than in the sleeping quarters where the overhead decks resemble a maze of white trunking interspaced at frequent intervals by punkah louvre valves through which a continuous supply of warm or cool air can be directed. Apart from such amenities for the troops as dry and wet canteens and their own barbers shop, the replanning of the *Georgic* has included facilities which will enable the military staff responsible for the organisation and running of the ship to do their work smoothly and expeditiously. These include:

A spacious orderly room in a centralised position on 'A' Deck. An internal broadcasting system which has involved the laying of miles of new wiring and the installation of hundreds of loud speakers in every part and corner of the ship. The fitting of scores of direction notices and deck 'guides' which will enable the men to move about the vessel quickly. The erection of cool and airy hospitals on one of the upper decks with adjacent rooms for R.A.M.C. personnel.

The commissioning of the *Georgic* as a troopship was one of the finest achievements in modern ship surgery and reconstruction.

It was on March 1, 1943, that the battle-scarred *Georgic* returned to Liverpool after her epic salvage and unescorted voyage home from Bombay. Immediately following her arrival, surveyors from the Admiralty and

Ministry of War Transport journeyed north to inspect the ship and report on the possibilities of her future service. Their survey revealed that before the ship could be re-commissioned a tremendous job of reconstruction would have to be done, for although the main hull had not sustained great damage and her machinery installation was practically in a normal condition, it would be necessary to remove in their entirety all the decks comprising the superstructure of the ship, the greater part of 'A' and 'B' decks and considerable sections of the lower decks. All the electrical and sanitary installations had been destroyed and would have to be replaced, the ship would have to be refurnished, and it would of course be essential to overhaul the main and auxiliary engines and machinery installation generally.

On March 16, 1943, at a meeting at the Ministry of War Transport in London, it was decided that the vessel should be reconstructed as a troopship and her previous owners, the Cunard White Star Company, were asked to take over the ship as managers on behalf of the Ministry.

Arrangements were then made for the *Georgic* to proceed from Liverpool to Belfast, where she arrived on March 19, lying to anchor in Bangor Bay, Belfast Lough, whilst final discussions took place regarding the shipbuilding firm to whom the task of reconstruction should be given. This was no easy decision to make as all British shipbuilding firms were working at high pressure on priority work. Vacant berths were non-existent. Labour was fully extended. The job practically reconstructing a 27,000 ton vessel was one which could not be accomplished in a matter of weeks. Urgent as it was, it would require to be fitted in with existing shipbuilding programmes.

The original builders of the *Georgic* had been Harland and Wolff of Belfast, and in view of their extensive knowledge of the vessel it was finally decided that they should be asked to undertake the work, and on May 24 the first gangs of workmen arrived on board. Before any part of the super-structure could be removed a great deal of deck gear, including boats, davits, fans, casings and piping had to be dismantled.

By June 3 this work had reached the stage when cutting of the steel decks and superstructure could start. In four days over 100 tons had been burned away, cut into small sections and loaded into a small coaster lying alongside the *Georgic*. Before cutting was finished this figure of 100 tons was to become 5,000 tons. So the work continued.

During those first weeks, due to the difficulty of obtaining a quayside berth, the *Georgic* was lying to anchor in Bangor Bay some 12 miles from Belfast and special arrangements had to be made to house and feed the workmen on board the ship. Early in July, however, a vacant berth adjacent to the shipbuilders' repair yard was found for her at No.3 quay in I Musgrave Channel, to which she moved on July 5.

By this time over 550 tons of steel had been removed and the ship was ready for the major operations which had to be carried out and for which the services of a floating crane were required. Amongst these tasks were cutting away and removal of two funnels, unshipping masts, removal of anti-aircraft and other guns, engine room silencers and tanks and deck houses. By the middle of August such progress had been made that the *Georgic* was ready for drydocking and on August 21 she was moved from her berth and entered the Thompson Graving Dock for examination and repair of her underwater parts, inspection and overhaul of her rudder and tail shafts, and the removal of her propellers.

The drydocking of the ship did not bring other demolition work to a halt and by the end of September, 1943, with no funnels, no masts and all her superstructure cut away and removed, all that remained of the original *Georgic* was her massive hull. Inside the hull large sections of the lower decks had been cut and the remaining sections supported by hundreds of shores; all internal fittings, wiring and many tons of debris had gone, her great machinery spaces had been opened up and scores of parts taken away for examination and renewal. To the lay mind, it seemed inconceivable that from this apparent shell a new ship could ever arise. To the experts in charge of the work, the turning point had been reached. For the first time their weekly progress report included the phrase:- "The restoration of the structure is in hand".

Many months of hard and unremitting labour were to pass before this work of restoration was to take visual shape. Intricate problems affecting the design of the new vessel had to be solved; labour problems caused by the pressing need for workmen on other more urgent jobs had to be overcome. But despite this the *Georgic* moved towards completion. By the end of May 1944, twelve months from the day when the first small gang of men arrived at the ship to begin the dismantling operation, nearly 2,000 men were employed on the job; the new superstructure was in position, trooping accommodation was being erected on the lower decks, the overhaul and renewal of machinery was nearing completion and throughout the vessel gangs of plumbers and electricians were laying and fitting miles of piping, cable and wiring.

During the summer and autumn, work was intensified to such an extent that by the end of October the exterior of the ship, including the stepping of the foremast and the erection of the single funnel, was almost complete and painters were busy transforming the great hull and upperworks into the uniform war-time grey. Work in the interior was also well advanced and it was now possible to gain some idea of the ultimate appearance of the ship.

Six weeks later, at the beginning of December, the

great task was completed. Stores had been taken on board, the crew had been signed-on. Everything was in readiness for trials. on Wednesday, December 13, 1944, the new *Georgic* once again under her own power left the Thompson quy for her trials. These took place during the next two days, after which she proceeded to Liverpool where sbe docked on Sunday December 17.

Nineteen months had passed since that day in March, 1943, when the *Georgic* had left Liverpool, a war worn casualty, her interior a pitiful shell of twisted girders, buckled plates and charred debris. In that time technical experts, aided by the British shipbuilding craftsmen, had achieved the seemingly impossible and out of the desolation that was the *Georgic,* created that which will stand for many years to come as the finest type of TROOPSHIP.

During the past twelve months she has been engaged as a troopship under Cunard White Star management carrying troops to and from Liverpool. The voyages have been mainly to the Middle East and India, calling at Naples, Algiers, Taranto, Port Said and Bombay. The *Georgic* which was the 27,300 ton motor vessel of the Cunard White Star Line and well known as a popular cruising liner on both sides of the Atlantic, has a length of 711 feet and abeam of 82'4". She was built at Harland & Wolff, Belfast, making her maiden voyage in June 1932.

DIMENSIONS:
Length (overall) ....711 feet
Breadth ....82.4 feet
Gross Tonnage 27,267

"GEORGIC"

Voyage Number	Date	Itinerary
117/21		Atlantic voyages
122	Apl.20/40-May 25/40	Liverpool, Clyde, Liverpool
123	May 27/40-June 18/40	Liverpool, Clyde, Andesfjord, Narvik, Greenock, Brest, St Nazaire, Liverpool
124	June 19/40-Jun 27/40	Liverpool - Liverpool
125	July 25/40-Aug 6/40	Liverpool, Clyde, Reykjavik, Clyde
126	Aug 11/40-Sept 6/40	Clyde, Halifax, Clyde, Liverpool
127	Sept 22/40-Jan 18/41	Liverpool, Clyde, Freetown Capetown, Aden, Port Tewfik, Durban, Capetown, Clyde, Liverpool
128	Jan 31/41-Mar 5/41	Liverpool, Bermuda, New York, Halifax, Liverpool
129	Mar 23/41-Apl 19/41	Liverpool, Halifax, Clyde
130	June 3/41	Glasgow, Port Tewfik

Bombed and set on fire — Vessel beached July 14/1941

"GEORGIC"
1940

Mar. 11. At 5pm requisitioned under Liner Requisition Scheme.

Apl. 19. Transferred to Charter Party T.97A.

1941

Jan. 25. At 10am transferred to Liner Requisition.

Mar. 18. Transferred to Charter Party T.97A.

July 14. Bombed and set on fire - vessel beached.

Nov. 30. Last day of hire.

1942

Sept. 3. Acquired by Government.

M.V. Georgic attacked by enemy aircraft at Port Tewfik (Suez) on July 14th 1941 and set on fire

She received a direct hit soon after 3am and was soon after ablaze. Dr O'Brien had a fire party place a hose on the starboard forehead bulk head door on 'B' deck to prevent the fire from reaching the Hospital on 'C' deck where crew, passengers and injured people were being medically cared for. If this steel door, which was becoming red hot, had collapsed, all these people would have perished as the upper structures of the ship were a blazing furnace and there was no other way of escape.

At the same time, considerable difficulty was experienced in getting the forehead gangway door on the starboard side of the ship open, this haing got jammed owing to the near misses the ship had been subjected to before being finally hit. This way of escape for a considerable time was cut off.

Eventually this door was opened and Dr O'Brien with the help of H. Deurdon, his dispenser, working entirely by themselves with a bosun's chair, lowered to waiting boats from other ships in the harbour, numbers of injured passengers, also men, women and children and in addition, about a hundred of the crew.

This took a considerable time and not till the last person was lowered to safety did either he or his dispenser leave the burning ship. It was then about 6.30-pm, being on

In flames — Suez Roads, 14th July 1941.
Courtesy of The University Archives, The University of Liverpool

this hazardous occupation for almost 3¹/2 hours. Many of the injured persons had to be very carefully handled. Some were lowered strapped into a Neil Robertson stretcher. The more nervous women and all the chldren were placed in blankets, which were securely tied at the top like a bundle.

In addition, Dr O'Brien constantly had to keep in touch with the fire party on 'B' deck bulkhead to see that their efforts were not relaxed in the slightest. This danger still existed; had this bulkhead door, even at this later hour caved in, the fire would have raged down.

"GEORGIC" SALVAGE

This is the story from July 1941 until early in 1945 of the Cunard White Star Line's motor passenger liner *Georgic* of 27,759 gross tons, built and engined in 1931 by Messrs. Harland & Wolff Ltd., at Belfast. It is a plain story of a wonderful achievement by British seafarers against all sorts of difficulties, delays and hazards of the sea and of the enemy. Unlike many stories of the sea war this one finishes upon a note of high accomplishment.

Month by month table of the Georgic's salvage and return to the United Kingdom:

Arrived Suez ....July 7, 1941

Attacked by enemy aircraft and set
ablaze ....July 14, 1941

Gutted by fire, beached with 18ft of water
in engine room ....July 16, 1941

Refloated and all arrangements made for
towing .... Oct 27, 1941

Left Suez ......, ... Dec 28, 1941

Arrived under tow at Port Sudan .... Jan 19, 1942

Arrived under tow at Karachi .... Mar 31, 1942

Sailed under her own power .... Dec 11, 1942

Arrived Bombay .... Dec 13, 1942

Sailed Bombay .... Jan 20, 1943

Arrived Liverpool .... March 1, 1943

How she withstood the enemy attack, was patched
up and safely brought home at an average speed of
16 knots is the theme of this article. Behind it lies
the quiet inflexible determination of a small number of
men who were resolved that the ship should not be allowed
to become a total loss. Chief among them are:

Capt. A.C. Greig, O.B.E., R.N.R.
Master of the Georgic
Mr D. Horsburgh
Chief Engineer
Capt. F.W. Manley
One of the owner's Marine Superintendents
Mr Douglas Ray
A Surveyor of Lloyd's Register
Commander A.S. Wheeler
Fleet Salvage Officer at Suez

There are of course many more, deck and engine-room officers, electricians, carpenters and others whose stout-hearted efforts contributed to the success of the undertaking. In all, nine men saw the job through from start to "finished with engines" at the ship's final destination.

Perhaps a word of praise should be given to the ship berself because the writer has Capt. Greig's word for it that the *Georgic* is a remarkably staunch, robust ship — one of the best that Harland & Wolff or any other builder has ever turned out in his view. "If she had been of ramshackle construction we would never have got her home", Capt. Greig said. One must not lose sight of the fact that this is a tribute from a Scot to a Northern Ireland firm of shipbuilders, and words of commendation rarely flow in that direction unless well and truly earned! As stated above, the *Georgic* arrived at Suez in July, 1941, with troops and 5,000 tons of military stores on board. The troops were immediately disembarked and unloading of the cargo was begun, the work being carried on night and day as the ship lay at anchor in Suez Roads. Two days later the air-raid warning sounded half-an-hour after midnight; work was stopped at once, the ship darkened, all anti-aircraft guns manned, bulkhead doors closed, fire-pumps and fire parties made ready for immediate action. At the time there were on board about 800 souls, this total being made up thus:-

Officers and crew 400

Passengers (evacuees from the Middle East) 136

R.N. Ratings 98

Service men 35

Arab Stevedores 130

To begin with, the attack by the enemy aircraft was directed at targets ashore, but after two hours had passed the *Georgic* was picked out for special attention. The first five bombs dropped fell in the water in the neighbourhood of the ship, but she was not harmed by any of them, none of the bombs being near enough to be classed as "near misses". Bomb No.6, however, came into this category, damaging the shell plating forward of the bridge on the port side, causing no little injury to the internal structure of the ship, and permitting the inrush of a considerable volume of water. The seventh bomb soon followed, a direct hit on the aft end of the sports deck; it pierced five decks before exploding in the after hold, fracturing the engine-room bulkhead about the level of D & E decks— in addition of course to doing much other damage by blast. At once the ship took fire, burning fiercely, and the fire spreading rapidly; within eight minutes the whole of the accommodation was a raging furnace fore and aft. The fire took hold on five decks simultaneously, apparently having been ignited at a number of points due to the blast from the last bomb, and proceeded along alleyways and galleries.

By this time, about 3.30am in addition to burning fiercely, the ship was making water rapidly, and listing to port, due to the damage done by the sixth bomb. The situation on board was obviously critical, particularly in view of the 800 persons exposed both to fire and enemy action, so Capt. Greig at once decided to shift the *Georgic* into shallower water. He deemed this the better course to follow in preference to trying to put out the fire by scuttling the ship and later events tend to show that this decision was the right and proper one.

Unfortunately, fire or blast or a combination of

both caused a complete breakdown of communication between the bridge and the engine-room, also between bridge and steering compartment. The ship therefore became unmanageable. An attempt was made to steer her by means of her screws, but this was foredoomed to failure because everything was "blacked-out" by the immense fall of smoke and smuts which blotted the surroundings from sight. In any event, smoke and flames soon drove everyone from the bridge and the ship had perforce to be left to her own devices. She went ashore on her own volition on the North Reef, not a spot which Captain Greig would have chosen, but not at what could rightly be called a bad place. The depth forward was 3½ fathoms and rather more aft with a rise and fall of tide of six feet; she settled with a maximum list of 17 degrees.

Before grounding, everyone on board had been assembled on the forecastle because the boat deck was unusable; from here survivors were taken off in such of the *Georgic's* own boats as had been got into the water, also in lighters and other small craft. By 5am the *Georgic* had been abandoned by all hands, still burning fiercely, with 18 feet of water in her main engine room. For two days she lay thus still on fire forward although other parts of the superstructure had completely burned out.

On the next day Capt. Greig led a small party on board to make a preliminary survey and what he saw can easily be left to the imagination; masses of debris, crumpled decks, corrugated steel plating; twisted bulkbeads and stanchions, dust, dirt and the charred remains of woodwork, carpets, fittings and fixtures wherever he looked, with an all pervading stench of fire. Later he was joined by two surveyors of Lloyd's Register who were temporarily commissioned in the Royal Corps of Naval Constructors and who were acting on behalf of the naval autborities. Meanwhile Capt. Manley and Mr Ray were on their way out to Suez: on their arrival further consultations took place with Commander Wheeler, Fleet Salvage Officer, formerly in the employ of the Liverpool & Glasgow Salvage Association, and with the representatives of the Flag Officer, as a result of which the decision was taken to commence salvage operations, and this work was quickly begun. First of all divers went down to plug all cracks and crevises, close any ports that might be open and generally make the hull as near water-tight as possible. Then pumps from the salvage steamer were put on board and set to work; pumping continued without interruption for nearly three weeks, care being exercised to pump out various compartments in proper sequence so as to avoid additional strain to the hull or cause any other fresh damage.

Successful efforts were made to dry out the main engine room as quickly as possible so as to get at the bilge pump; as soon as it was accessible it was sent ashore for cleaning and overhaul while the salvage pumps were kept at work and the ship was duly floated - an inert mass of twisted steel, dead machinery and tons of debris.

How was this relic of a once-fine ship to be revitalised? was the next question, and the answer came in the form of — a farm generating set! Of 40 h.p. it was purchased locally: it was of American manufacture and bad been designed to generate power for any of the purposes to which an up-to-date farmer might apply electric energy. This set was installed in the remains of the cabin dining saloon, connected electrically with the overhauled motor of the bilge pump, and set to work.

Manfully this unorthodox fit-up did its job; it kept the ship dry, or dry enough to permit of the removal of the salvage pumps. During the role of the time that the *Georgic* was being prepared for towing this agricultural emergency generating station was kept hard at work; it ran without a falter. Meanwhile the hull was made as water-tight as possible, the main task being to build a cement

*The 'Georgic' after she was refloated — badly damaged
by the bombing*

Lying beached at Tewfik

box inside the damaged shell plating on the port side. This was done but due to the lack of facilities at Suez it was not wholly satisfactory, and during subsequent heavy weather permitted the ingress of water as will be described later on.

Consideration was next given to the problem of towing the ship to the nearest port where temporary repairs could be effected: towage of a ship of the size of the *Georgic* is no small task under any circumstances, and it was made much more difficult because nobody would be allowed to travel in the ship. Without power or control for steering she would be just like an enormous log wallowing in the sea, at the mercy of wind and weather. Several shipowners who had ships available at Suez declined to allow their vessels to try to tow the *Georgic* to Karachi because of the damage that the towing ship might sustain.

However, arrangements were finally made for the *Clan Campbell* to tow, with the *City of Sydney* made fast by means of a long hawser to the *Georgic* astern to steer her. The *Clan Campbell* is a twin-screw, geared turbine steamer, 463 feet long, 7255 gross tons, owned by Clan Line Steamers Ltd., and built, in 1937 by the Greenock Dockyard Co., Ltd. *The City of Sydney* is a single-screw turbine steamer 454 feet long, 6986 gross tons owned by Ellerman Lines Ltd., and built in 1930 by Messrs. Workman Clark & Co., Ltd.

Towing began on December 28th, 1941, and steady progress was made for some time at about 6½ knots until off Port Sudan. The wind was freshening until it reached gale force and a big sea running, a combination which made the *Georgic* almost unmanageable. In addition, Capt. Greig on board the *Clan Campbell* saw that the *Georgic* was taking a list so he decided to put into Port Sudan to shelter from the weather and to investigate the trouble. This was later discovered to have been caused by the cement box built at Suez weakening.

Both the *Clan Campbell* and the *City of Sydney* had done yeoman service in handling their big and ungainly charge; Capt. Greig is full of praise for everything that the masters, officers and crews of these two ships did to help him in his heavy task. On arrival at Port Sudan those two ships were ordered to proceed on their interrupted voyages and Capt. Greig said good-bye to them with a sensation of genuine regret.

For six weeks the *Georgic* lay at Port Sudan getting patched up again and waiting for a suitable towing ship to be procured. At last the *Recorder* was detailed to tow and a tug to steer. The *Recorder* is a reciprocating engined steamer of 5982 tons, 420 feet long, owned by the Charente Steamship Co., Ltd., and built in 1930 by Messrs. Cammell, Laird & Co., Ltd. When all was ready the convoy sailed with Capt. Greig and Capt. Manley.

It soon became evident that the tug assigned to the task was much too light for the purpose; particularly in anything approaching a breeze. While on tow to Karachi the weather worsened and the tug either broke away from the *Georgic* or cast off; Capt. Greig does not know which occurred only that it was the last he saw of the tug. A steamer belonging to the British India Steam Navigation Co.Ltd. , fortunately happened to be near at hand and she was connected up to the stern of the *Georgic* and progress was continued at about 4½knots. The British India Steam Navigation Co. steamer was the *Haresfield*. No further incidents were reported, Karachi being reached on 31 March, 1942: one can well imagine the feelings of relief that must have been shared by all concerned after they had finished so successfully this difficult and dangerous feat of navigation.

As soon as the ship had berthed at Karachi the big job of effecting temporary repairs was commenced. There was an enormous task to be faced in each department — on deck, in the engine rooms and in the stewards' department. Practically nothing usable remained.

It is impossible to attempt to catalogue the innumerable tasks that were accomplished but in general terms it can be said that extensive repairs were carried out to the electrical equipment—the *Georgic* was an 'all-electric' ship—the main and auxiliary engines were cleaned and overhauled, electric motors dried out, debris removed, burnt paint replaced and so on. Much of the work was done under the direct control and supervision of the ship's staff who engaged such labour as they required for the purpose, and for whose accommodation a canteen was built ashore alongside the ship. Local firms such as Messrs. Herman Mohatta & Co., Messrs. Carstairs & Cumming and also Karachi Port Trust lent invaluable aid. Temporary accommodation was built of timber on 'A' deck for the Lascar crew, a mess room for officers and another for ratings were constructed on 'C' deck, officers' cabins were made habitable, running hot and cold water was reinstated, the ship was 'degaussed' afresh and so on.

The general standard of all this work performed by native labourers was very high. First of the ship's machinery to be brought back to life was one of the main generating sets, then the various auxiliaries followed in sequence - air, water and oil pumps, etc. Then the main engines were turned over by means of compressed air, and after all was found to be in reasonable shape, extensive dock trials were run with the ship firmly moored to the quayside.

One cause of discomfort and a potential source of danger was caused by the fact that the asbestos lagging around various exhaust pipes had absorbed quantities of oil, while the level of water and oil fell in the engine room during pumping operations. When the related pipes became heated during trials of the engines, the lagging gave off clouds of smoke and oily vapour, this being both noxious and a potential fire risk. Many little delays like this were overcome; irritating and vexatious as they were, they

At sea bound for Australia. A wave has just broken over the fo'castle.
October 1949

Three young crew members on the beach in Australia.

Proceeding to No. 3 Musgrave Channel
(Courtesy of Liverpool University Archives)

Aft end of 'A' Deck (from Promenade Deck)
(Courtesy of Liverpool University Archives)

Nicknamed "Super Trooper" — shifting to Victoria Wharf for stores.
(Courtesy of Liverpool University Archives)

'Georgic' on Trials, Belfast Lough. Dec. 1944
(Courtesy of Liverpool University Archives)

merely served to strengthen everyone's determination to see the job through as quickly as possible.

At Karachi engine room ratings were signed on, while deck hands and stewards were brought from Bombay.

At last the great day came when Capt. Greig and Capt. Manley decided that the ship was fit to proceed to sea again under her own power, and accordingly the *Georgic* sailed for Bombay for drydocking. Compasses were adjusted, and degaussing ranged, various other minor adjustments made, faults rectified and so on. Otherwise there were few incidents either on deck or down below with the ship 'motoring' at an easy 10-11 knots.

On arrival at Bombay the *Georgic* was dry-docked to ascertain the extent of the damage to the under water portions of the hull, also to check the alignment and paint the hull, examine propellers and rudder as well as effect permanent repairs to the damaged shell plating. As might well be expected from the rough treatment by fire and grounding, the hull was found to be twisted and sagged, though not to any great extent. The fact that the tail-shaft bearings ran without developing excessive heat indicates that the twisting of the hull was not excessive.

New shell plates were fitted in way of the damage on the port side, with welded seams and screwed connections to new stiffeners which were themselves welded to the structure of the hull. Then a cement backing was applied. According to Capt. Greig this repair was immensely strong. The result of the investigation into the condition of the hull showed that it was fully strong enough to withstand all normal strains, a tribute to the staunchness of the work of Belfast's craftsmen. At Bombay the dry-docking etc., was executed by the Mazagon Dock Co. who, like the firms at Karachi, placed the whole of their resources and experience at the disposal of the ship.

Before leaving Bombay 5,000 tons of Indian pig-iron was loaded into the holds, disposed equally at the fore and aft ends of the ship. This ballasted the ship in addition to earning for her a freight of £10,000: on 20 January, 1943, the *Georgic* sailed from Bombay, calling at Capetown for stores.

The voyage home was made at an average speed of 16 knots compared with a designed speed of 18 knots. This was a remarkably fine performance. Most of the engineers had been in the ship for a long time and knew her engines intimately. To them for their knowledge, skill and perseverance the owners and indeed the whole country are greatly indebted. The voyage home occupied six weeks and was made unescorted, the ship relying on her speed and defensive armament had she been attacked. Such, fortunately however, was not the case.

Much more could be written, and no doubt will be written in due course, concerning this great achievement: a whole book would do no more than adequate justice, to the *Georgic* and to the men who got her home. The Journal of Commerce and Shipping Telegraph is proud to have this opportunity of publishing this much of the *Georgic's* saga; on behalf of the whole of the British shipping press we congratulate Capt. Greig, his deck and engineer officers and his staff for their patience, skill and courage; we thank the owners of the *Georgic*, Cunard's White Star Ltd., for their co-operation in making possible the writing of this story.

Charlie Attwell from Queensland, Australia who in November 1940 left the H.M.A.S.*Voyager* after serving in the Mediterranian Sea, was being sent to the U.K. as part of the crews to take up their posting on the new 'N' class Destroyers — Napier, Nizam, Nestor, Norman and Nepal.

He was sent to Port Tewfik at the southern end of the Suez Canal. There he went aboard the *Georgic* which sailed to Durban and picked up more troops, then sailed to Scotland. Unescorted as the *Georgic* was at that time, she was the fastest motor vessel afloat. Charles and two others, named Arty and Harold Davis, were part of the guns crew who manned the guns mounted on the stern —"6 inch guns they were."

Afterwards, they left the *Georgic* on the next trip back to Tewfik. She was loading Italian prisoners when she was hit by a bomb and ran aground. We assumed she was lost, then after the war "I couldn't believe my eyes when the old girl herself came steaming into Melbourne packed with emigrants!"

C.E. Eldridge R.N. of Duncrag, Western Australia tells of his experiences on the *Georgic*, "the story goes back to World War II.

"I was in the R.N. and serving in the Far East. The war in Europe had ended, and the Yanks and the British were going to finish off the Jap.I, and with a lot more, had taken enough from them. I still have the scars, and nightmares to prove it, what with being bombed, shot at etc., etc., I can never forget.

Getting back to the *Georgic*, my family were all builders, and the first men to come out of the forces were builders — someone had to put U.K. back to right!

My father applied for my release as he had so much work on and not the manpower, so the powers that be, said to me you are going home. It was no fun being shunted around for thousands of miles till I got to Bombay, in India. There I boarded the *Georgic*, well one ship was the same as any to me. I knew the drill. The war was still on. My first impression when I went below was to see all the buckled plates. To myself I said "this heap has coffed a packet sometime or the other." It looked as if she had 'collected' a torpedo.

There were quite a few R.N. blokes on board taking passage to U.K. and we kept quiet about how the damage was caused. There was still the Japanese subs to think about. Being one of the 'elite force' about which the story has never yet been told, I was asked to go below to sort out 'some trouble'. I went down. There were a couple of dozen blokes in a gangway, one was a big bloke who wanted to take over the job of being first into the mess deck for 'tucker'.

Well, I told this mountain he has to line up same as everyone else. "What the hell are you" he said, and to this I replied "I am only obeying orders, line up like everyone else you will all be served". Then out it came. He was the great Freddy Mills the boxer — like Vera Lynn who was also on board, he had come out to do shows etc."

Mary Carol Rhind who's father was a Army Gunner on the *Georgic* told the troops were wakened every morning to the record "Tennament Symphony" sung by Tony Martin.

Harry West never did sail on the *Georgic* but recalls seeing her twice during the war in different parts of the world. He was serving with the 1st Battalion Royal Sussex Regiment in 1940-1941 in Port Suez at the Shell Refinery when he saw the *Georgic* beached in shallow water. His regiment was then moved up to the Western Desert where he was captured by the Italians and became a prisoner of war at Benghazi.

After spending 1 1/2 years in various camps in Italy, on September 8th, 1943 the Germans over-ran their camp and they were all taken into Germany to spend another 1 1/2 years, until early in 1945. He escaped from the line of march with another fellow, and managed to get to Odessa on the Black Sea.

After about 4 weeks, a convoy of ships supplying the Russians arrived at the Port of Odessa, bringing new uniforms for all the escaped P.O.W.s that were there — 150 of them at the time.

When they left Odessa and put out to sea, one of the ships in front of his ship the *Highland Prince,* was the M.V. *Georgic* and he saw it all the way to Egypt.

THE IMMIGRANT RUN

In December 1949 the Georgic left Liverpool carrying 2002 passengers and 486 crew bound for Melbourne then Sydney. Calling at Port Said and Port Aden. From Sydney she was to sail to Batavia. Chartered by the Netherlands Ministerie to pick up 1976 service personnel and their families, together with their baggage; carriage was to Amsterdam or Rotterdam.

Messing to be provided on the scale of 5/- per day average. The standard of messing to be graded at ship discretion in consultation with the Liaison Officer.

Officers, W.O.s, Sergeants and Civilians were supplied with bed linen and towels on the usual Civilian Passenger Standard. Other ranks were supplied at the ship's discretion.

It was agreed the Charterer will embark as part of the total number of passengers. One or more suitable persons who would act as Liaison officers to the ship's personnel and to provide a Baggage Master if found necessary.

Troops were informed that fatigue parties of troops would assist in the Galley or in helping to keep and tidy that part of the ship used by the troops. The same sort of arrangement was made with immigrants only more on a volunteer basis. A boxing ring was erected on the open deck and competitions were organised which were found to be very popular both with the troops and immigrants. A good crowd of spectators was guaranteed at all matches and the ship's crew were invited to take part. On one voyage a ship's cook completely shattered the morality of the troops by knocking out the Army champion. Here were also the usual other deck games and films were shown on the open deck.

D. Cross of Alphington, Victoria, Australia tells of "My first sight of the *Georgic* was in 1942. She was resting on the bottom of Port Said harbour. We were told she got hit in convoy and was sunk to put out the fire.

Imagine our surprise when emigrating to Australia we were booked to travel on the *Georgic*. Our journey was troop ship style. Males and females were segregated. My wife was up forward on 'C' Deck in Cabin A with nine others. I was left on 'C' Deck with 7 others — males. Meal time was chaotic, we sat along tables seating 20 people and the toilets and showers were communal. I can't remember how many was on board, but a hell of a lot. If you managed to get a seat on the upper deck and you walked to the rail, you lost your seat!

The shortage of seating could be partly blamed on a group of boys travelling under the Big Brother Scheme who were allegedly seen throwing deck chairs over the stern of the ship, which were sucked into the ship's props, smashing the chairs to splinters. How long this had been going on for nobody seemed to know, or maybe the boys could have been charged with the more serious offence of maliciously damaging the ship. Port Line Ltd. who acted a agents for Cunard White Star Ltd. wrote to Cunard as follows:

The *Georgic* arrived here on the 11th November. Dry docked at the Captain Cook Dock on the 14th November. Left dry dock on the 18th November and berthed at No.8 Wharf, Woolloomocoo, until the following day, when she sailed at 11am, having had a spare propeller fitted replacing a damaged propeller which occured on the inward voyage. How was the propeller damaged?

Since the departure of the *Georgic* from Sydney it was found two waiters missed the ship and nothing more was heard of them. Then two stowaways appeared on board and gave themselves up. One was a labourer .from Liverpool, the other a motor mechanic from Runcorn. Not being entitled to the repatriation rule, they were put to work in the galley to pay their passage to Liverpool where the immigration authorities would decide what and if any action would be taken.

As the ship had left two catering staff in hospital in Sydney with illness, plus the two waiters who missed the ship, the extra hands were welcome.

The *Georgic* was always willing to belp repatriate seamen, as seamen in distress. An example was on a voyage from Liverpool in January 1949. Five Australian seamen were repatriated per the *Georgic* and arrangements had been made to sign them off at Sydney. They were all found work as Assistant Cooks for which they would be paid at the seamens' rate. Another man ex the *Fort Cadotte*, a New Zealander, was not entitled to repatriation and was signed on as galley boy. Requests were sent to the New Zealand Government from officers from the *Georgic* to assist this young man in his onward movements from Sydney to New Zealand. I found myself on the beach after missing ship but I'll write about it later in the book.

I would just like to mention at this point about the *Georgic* changing colours from battleship grey to the colours of Cunard White Star. I did find that she was applied with a full coat of anti-foul-paint ('Red Hand'). She also had a coat of boot topping while in Dry Dock in Sydney. But the fact remains some photographs show her in grey and some in Cunard White Star colours. I certainly know she was in the latter colours in 1955, but alas, having interviewed many deck crew who sailed on her, I never received a definite date of change.

In December 1950 **George Parker** of Queensland, Australia, then 13 years old was due to sail from London to Melbourne with his parents, brother, sister and grandfather.

At the time there were major problems with strikes and one ship was held up indefinitely. "We were put on a train and sent to Liverpool, there we boarded the M. V. *Georgic*. Up to that time she was doing the Liverpool to New York run. As migrants we found our selves lucky to have such a wonderful trip. We had a shortage of crew but they looked after us. A ship that size was a wonderful adventure to a youngster. I never tired of playing games or exploring her.

We left Liverpool December 4th, 1950 and arrived in Melbourne on January 4th, 1951. We came through the Suez Canal when the Arabs were starting their anti-British push. And we had an army escort between Port Said and Port Aden."

The first words from **Mrs.E.O'Shea** from Greensborough, Victoria, when I asked of her memories of the *Georgic* were "what a blast from the past". She, with her parents sailed on the homeward bound *Georgic* in 1951 from Melbourne to Liverpool. There were only a few hundred passengers on board and nearly as many crew, also on board were the crew of a cargo boat which had come to grief off the Queensland Coast. Mrs. O'Shea, then seventeen years of age, entered the ships' Beauty Competition and came first 'albeit only 4 entered'.

In June 1952 **David Wilcox** his wife and baby daughter sailed from Southampton to New York as immigrants, as were the rest of the passengers, first calling at Nova Scotia to drop off Canadian immigrants.

"I have to be quite candid about this," said Mr. Wilcox. "The accommodation was terrible, families were split up to different parts of the ship, our cabin was below the water line so there was no daylight. Laundry facilities were nil, washing was done in wash-hand basins, an my wife used to hang up the nappies in the cabin, and then sleep on them to air them. There was also head lice amongst some of the children. The food was very good, but as you can imagine, most people were still rationed in most countries, and once the food was put on the tables it was gone in seconds. We were on the first serving of breakfast, and once it was over, the passengers used to start queueing for morning 'Bovril'. I must admit the crew were marvellous to us under the circumstances."

Pushed up together like peas in a pod
Eight of us here by the good grace of God
Snug in a cabin that lies on Deck 'E'.
Two Scots men, two Yorkies, two Geordies and we
I from the north, and he from the west
Eight of us here, would be eight of the best.

Written by an immigrant on the Georgic on its way to Australia.

On Saturday May 14th, 1955, the Liverpool Echo newspaper printed the following:

"Waiters walk off stops sailing, *Georgic* is held up 80 men quit."

The 27,000 tonne vessel *Georgic* was unable to sail from Prince's Landing Stage, Liverpool, last night, when some eighty members of the ship's catering department walked off the ship in protest against shortage of staff.

They complained that with more than sixty men short in the dining room, twenty five boys, most of them on their first sea trip, were sent aboard to help out. In addition, notices were posted on four decks asking passengers, all emigrants to Australia, to help the catering department at a fee of 10s. a day! which was more than the boys would get. Later, some of the seamen walked off the ship in sympathy with the stewards.

Due to sail for Sydney at 8pm with 1,800 passengers, the liner was first held up, as fresh water had yet to be taken on. She could, however, have sailed at 9pm, if the catering staff had returned. The evening meal, last night was served by the remainder of the catering staff, helped by bedroom stewardesses, some of the passengers helped with washing up.

The reason for the shortage of staff, was said by both Cunard officials and strikers to be a dearth of catering staff in Liverpool. The Cunard Liner Saxonia sailed on Thursday, seven men short in the catering department.

The M.V.*Georgic* had had more than her fair share of trouble before arriving in Liverpool to carry 1800 hundred emigrants to Australia. Having been bombed by enemy aircraft in 1942, she was beached in shallow water, then raised and towed by a tug and cargo boat to Bombay where repairs were carried out to enable her to limp back to Belfast for major repairs and a refit.

With one funnel instead of her normal two, and minus her front mast, she returned to troop carrying. In 1949 she was chartered by the Australians from the Ministry of Transport and War, to carry emigrants from England to Australia. On the 13 May 1955 she arrived in Liverpool, the 1800 emigrants were there waiting, having arrived at Riverside Railway station by train, or at the Princes Landing Stage by car and taxi, the huge embarkation halls being where they checked in to have their sailing documents checked. Luggage was sorted, then clearly marked, with their names and the sleeping quarters they were allocated to. They then boarded the ship,

The 'Georgic' now ready for the Australian run

Some of these boy waiters sailed on the Georgic on the Australia
run. Arrowed is the auther.

41

with the help of the ships' shore gang stewards, who carried
their luggage. _____

I was working in the shore gang, on a ship called
Media, docked in the Huskisson Dock, Liverpool. I had
worked for the Cunard Line since completion of a six week
course, at the sea training school at Gravesend.

I was ordered to report to Head Office, Cunard
Buildings, Liverpool immediately. Arriving at the Catering Department I was told to gather my gear from home
then report to the Chief Steward on the M.V. *Georgic*,
Princes Landing Stage, Liverpool.

I arrived on board the ship at 2pm. and after signing
on, I went below to my assigned quarters (The Glory Hole)
where I found amongst nine cabin mates, two mates I had
sailed with before who had also been short noticed. Of course
you did not have to join the ship but if you refused you
had a good chance of National Service in the Armed Forces
for two years. The two shipmates I will call John and Mike.

I soon realised all was not right, and asked John
what the problem was. He told me the Union official has
informed us we are about to sail with 65 men short in
the Catering Department and there was talk of a walk
off (strike) and that rumour was spreading of agents
appointed by Cunard to call at local ale houses to muster
up any person willing to sail at short notice with a
Discharge Book or not. A meeting was taking place in the
'Pig and Whistle' and so we made our way up there.

As we entered, a show of hands was taking place
to find how many was prepared to grab their gear from
below and walk ashore in protest. I recall we, the boy
waiters, all put our bands up but were told to "Stay out of
it, you're too young!" This we did.

One of the Stewards who walked off told a Reporter
from the 'Daily Post' that the Catering Department had
been 65 men short in the afternoon, then 25 boys (of which

I was one) were sent to the ship to make up the numbers —
"they are all under 18, most of them on their first trip
and getting £10. 12s.6d. per month." Another protester
added: "We (the stewards) get £26.10s. a month but some
of the boys will have to do the same job we do. It is not fair
they should get such low wages and we know that this is
the first time passengers have been asked to assist the
catering staff at the rate of 10s per day. They will be getting
more money than the boys."

Before long the protesting stewards were gathering
on the Landing Stage, carrying their belongings, then it
started raining and some decided to go home. The Chief
and Second Steward made their way down the Gangway
from the ship followed by the Catering Superintendant
(C.S.) to speak to the leader of the strikers. The C.S.
assured the leading striker, that no person without a
Seaman's Book had been signed on and that he had tried
to get more stewards without success. We offered the
passengers 10s. per day and have now withdrawn the offer.
The strike leader, who was now joined by a Union official
asked the Chief Steward

"Can you confirm this?"

"Yes, I can," be replied.

He then went on to pay all boy waiters the same
wages as the full waiters. I was pleased to hear the promise
and so of course were all the other boy waiters. My normal
duties would be to assist a full waiter. Now I would be doing
all the waiting on my own albeit that we would not be
offering a Silver Service and I knew we would require
some assistance from passengers. I always considered myself
lucky to be employed by Cunard White Star; every crew
member was trained to a high standard, frequent
inspections of crew quarters were carried out by Senior
Officers. One had to keep one's self smart at all times.' If the
Chief told you to get your hair cut, you did it without
question.

But of course the Chief Steward had no authority to discipline passengers for being untidy and a few of them were scruffy to say the least. However, they were a minority. The Liverpool Echo newspaper read that night...

"Strike on liner is settled, two promises to stewards, extra staff"

The strike on board the 27,000 ton *Georgic* ended today, when Stewards were promised that no man would incur any penalties, and that any boy doing adult work would be paid at the appropriate rate.

Early today Company officials and officers of National Union of Seamen had a conference on board.

A spokesman for the Company said. "We will definitely get the extra crew."

The Stewards met at 1pm. and appointed a three man deputation to go on board and inspect the names of those who had joined the crew. When the Stewards' deputation was satisfied that enough men had been taken on, they decided to return on two conditions —no victimisation and that boys would be paid the full men's rate.

At 1.50pm a letter agreeing to these conditions was read to the men by their spokesman. He hold them it was signed by the Captain of the ship. The men said they wanted the letter signed by a representative of the National Union of Seamen. An official signed the letter in full view of the men using the back of a colleague as a writing desk. The men then said they wanted the letter by a representative of the Shipping Federation. Their spokesman went back on board where the letter was signed by the representative of the Shipping Federation, who also confirmed that all the vacancies had been filled that morning.

Passengers on board washed dishes and waited at table while a decision was awaited from the stewards. Some passengers found the enforced idleness tedious and wished they might go ashore, but scores of others who had volunteered to help in the kitchens and in the dining rooms were having a wonderful time. Among these immigrants was a ten year old girl from Grimsby who was helping a stewardess to arrange rows and rows of tea pots ready for the next meal. A thirteen year old girl from Oxford washed hundreds of dishes during her turn at the sink.

"It's great fun, we never have all these dishes to wash at home." she grinned.

Many of the woman emigrants recruited their husbands as well as children into the volunteer corps. The men laughed and talked as they laid the tables for lunch which had earlier been cleared by youngsters. With their wives, they swept the floors and also took their turn at the sinks with the shore crew. Said Mrs. Harrison, a widow from South Wales, emigrating with her seventeen year old daughter,

"I certainly didn't anticipate housework, but it's certainly better than sitting around and we are enjoying it; someone has to do it or we would not get any food."

As children raced all over the ship, their parents queued for drinks, sweets and cigarettes. So much orange and lemonade was being drunk by the hundreds of youngsters that extra supplies of soft drinks were ordered because it was feared that the supplies scheduled for the voyage would not be sufficient and cases of soft drinks were carried on board from delivery vans on the Stage.

A cinema show and other entertainments were being organised to occupy the emigrants' families. There have been no complaints and scores have volunteered to help out. Hearing that the *Georgic* was still at the Landing Stage, relatives who said goodbye to their families yesterday hurried to the Stage hoping to catch a last glimpse of their families.

Among them was a lady from Liverpool who yesterday gave her daughter a last kiss and a hug and hoping for a chance of seeing her again, she scanned the decks as they all did; some were lucky, some were not. Another couple from Edinburgh who had stayed the night in a Liverpool hotel, were informed as they ate breakfast that the *Georgic* had not sailed yet. They rushed down to the Landing Stage, and were delighted to catch sight of their daughter, her husband and grandchildren, before catching the train back to Scotland.

British seamen all over were perturbed at this time, as many ships were sailing under-crewed. Liners were particularly hit and many had to cancel voyages. Added to this, the tug men were on strike which choked up the docks and river. It was only the day previous to the sailing of the *Georgic*, the tugs returned to work, then for the Company to offer passengers 10s. per day to help run the ship was an insult to trained and qualified men.

Albeit that the emigrants were only paying £10 fare, the balance was made up by the Australian and British Governments. Could one imagine asking the passengers on the *Queen Mary* or the *Coronia* to help out in the kitchens for 10s. per day? The fact of the matter seems that the Company over stretched its man-power.

As soon as everybody was on board, the gangways were lifted. Casting off, the ship moved to mid river with the aid of two tugs. On 14th May the ship sailed for Australia, passing the inward arrival of the Manx ferry M .V *Tynwald*. The clock on the Liver Building said 6.30pm. Both tugs having disengaged, made their way toward Birkenhead.

The ship moved along at 8 knots; the passengers still lined the decks waving their hands to any person ashore who waved to them; then passing the chimney stacks nicknamed the ugly sisters, on towards the lightship. The lights on the big wheel in New Brighton's Leasure ground were now flashing in an array of different colours. The Irish Sea lay ahead.

Ships from all nations lay at anchor in the bay waiting for dock space, to unload their cargoes.

Then the Pilot boat arrived alongside to take off the pilot, his task now completed in steering the ship down the proper channels. A cargo boat, so rusted its name could not be recognised, passed on its way up river.

The ship's speed now increased to 18 knots as she headed for the open sea.

The first Port of Call was Cobh in Southern Ireland to pick up two Irish families who were also voyaging to Australia. I recall the ship dropping anchor off shore to await the arrival of the tender boat which arrived within a couple of minutes. When all were safe on board, the ship raised anchor and set sail for Gibraltar and the Mediterranean Sea. The Stewards were preparing the tables for dinner in the large saloon restaurant capable of seating 650 diners or more. I was to wait on Table Nos. 14 and 15 — ten diners to each table with two sittings.

I had received a list of passengers who I would be looking after, and decided to call every passenger Sir or Madam until I got to know them. As they were shown to their respective table by the Head Waiters I wished all my diners "Good Evening", then took their orders. The meal went without incident except for Jack Wilson's son who, feeling sea sick made his way at speed towards the saloon door only to collide with a waiter carrying a full tray of steam pudding and custard which covered both boy and waiter. Jack Wilson and his family came from my home town; they were emigrating to Perth.

The ship had crossed the turbulent Bay of Biscay while they slept, and was now heading for the Straits of Gibraltar.

The sea was now quite calm. The temperature was rising which pleased everybody, being able to go up on deck to enjoy the sunshine. The sight of passing ships bound for the English Channel and further, was always a pleasant sight so too was the display of dolphins as they raced along with the ship.

The distant shores of Portugal and Spain were just visible through a haze and the sky was becoming bluer by the minute.

Breakfast was over and so the women set about their washing of personals in the wash rooms on 'C' Deck. Problems arose when some items of clothing were blown overboard into the sea. The sight of the drying washing hung all over the ship was not a pleasant sight, which must have displeased the ship's bosun and indeed the skipper. The ship did have a launderette which was totally inadequate. Most of the emigrants were poor people and had a limited amount of clothing, so washing clothes was a daily routine. The ship's crew had their own launderette service, employing some twenty personnel whose duty it was to clean any item of clothing, plus of course the ship's linen.

As more and more washing vanished over the ship's side, tempers becoming a bit short and it was decided to construct cages on the open decks. Allocation of times and spaces was organised and the drying problem was sorted. On a ship the size of the *Georgic*, it was possible not to see a person you knew, unless or course they worked in your department, or slept in or near your cabin. And so it was with passengers — the only passengers you got to know were those you catered for. In my case that meant the twenty people on my tables.

Ship's crew where not allowed to mix with passengers in their cabins nor in the Staterooms' bars except in the capacity of their duties. John found this out to his cost; being invited to a drink in the late bar by a young lady

Passengers wait for the Film Show
On board the 'Georgic' — October 1949

First glance at Australia

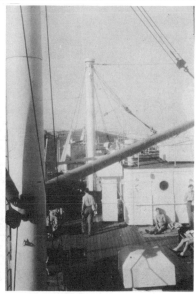

Ron Woolston, Tom Hunter, Harry Rae, Charlie Lynch
playing Bullboard on board 'Georgic' Oct. 1949

Passing through Suez Canal on board 'Georgic'
October 1949

Boxing Ring on board 'Georgic' en-route to Australia, October 1949

from his table, he had finished serving the evening meal. He had gone down to the Glory Hole to change clothing from his Steward's outfit into his civvy clothes to avoid being spotted by a Master of Arms. John, having met his date, took her into the passenger bar, finding a table in the corner. He went to the bar for drinks, returning to the table after being warned the M.A.s were on the look out. John and his girlfriend were into their second drink when from the corner of his eye he spotted an M.A. making straight for his table. The game was up. John was ordered back to the crews' side, after being ordered to be outside of the Chief Steward's office the following morning. The outcome was, John was fined a day's pay.

Many crew members were caught at this game — not surprising really as there were a lot of attractive girls on board and passengers were frequently making use of the "Pig 'n Whistle" without reprisal.

'The Pig & Whistle" — Georgic 1945

On the morning of 26th May I was woken by the noise of the ship's engines as she edged ber way into the quayside at Port Said. The ship would be here for a short stay to take on stores including one ton of ice cream. Back home in Liverpool, whoever had ordered the ice cream could not have checked on the number of children on board.

The 'Georgic' at Port Said

No shore leave was allowed. Some twenty ships from all over, the *Georgic* being the largest, gathered to convoy through the Suez Canal. The deck hands set up high-power water hoses on both sides of the ship to discourage thieving Arabs boarding the ship from their small sailing craft. They would come alongside the ship, climb up their masts and after greasing their bodies would slide through any open port hole. Cotton bed sheets, they particularly wanted. Signs were put on the decks of the ship warning passengers and crew that heavy fines would be imposed on any persons' swapping their bed sheets for fancy goods offered by the Arabs.

I acquired a pig skin suitcase from the 'bum boats' which sailed alongside the ship. I can't recall how much I paid but I do recall pulling up the suitcase on a rope then, being satisfied with the deal, lowered the payment down to the bum boat. The heat below deck was very intense; the vent system was totally inadequate. The saloons and lounges however were air conditioned.

I wrote home telling my mother of my increase in wages and that I had increased my weekly allotment to her and that I did not expect much in the way of tips, as a lot of passengers had less than we had. I must say I had great admiration for the immigrants. Here they were, venturing half-way across the world with a dream.

The voyage through the Suez Canal took twelve hours passing by a small town called Ismailla. The Trustee Arabs on board now disembarked carrying with them as much food as they could scrounge from the galleys. The *Georgic* then sailed into the Gulf of Suez, then into the Red Sea.

The heat of the sun was now so intense, the sick bay was full of heat-exhausted passengers, especially children who played on the open decks in singlets and shorts —some wearing sandals, some bare-footed. Sun rashes were common and in some cases sun stroke. Mothers were allowed to take children down by the ship's cold rooms to enable them to breath more easily. Canvas life boats were erected on the open deck, then filled with water for the children to play in. The ship's tannoys bellowed warning to passengers to stay out of the ferocious sun. Rumour had it that two babies had died from heat exhaustion. I cannot confirm or deny this. The ship's doctor and his aids certainly had a full time job on their bands. Thank goodness for the well equipped ship's hospital and dispensary, and thanks to the many women who assisted the medical staff in nursing the sick.

I had my first fall out at dinner. A young lad emigrating with his Irish parents was forever changing his mind over his meals and calling out to me "TATTIES, TATTIES, TATTIES, I want more TATTIES."

I knew the lad meant potatoes. He would also watch what was being served on the next table, and would say "I don't want this, I want what they're getting."

Added to this, the lad's hands were always filthy dirty. I forgot my position and told the lad's father to control his son. The father said he was going to report me for insolence then changed his mind.

"Thank God", it would have cost me a day's pay.

The Georgic arrived at Port Aden on the last day of May. She was secured to two huge pontoons off-shore. Shore leave was permitted for the crew albeit that the ship would only be here for 2½ hours. Crew trouble erupted when a crew member entered a bar in the town which was packed with not only *Georgic* crew but crews from other ships. He said a bell boy from the *Georgic* had been accused

Our first view of Aden from the 'Georgic'

of stealing from one of the stores and was getting a beating from a crowd of Arab youths. Twenty or thirty men charged out of the bar and down to the trouble spot. The men attacked the Arab youths. More Arabs got involved some wielding clubs and knives. The *Georgic* crew members would have been badly beaten, they were so out numbered, if it was not for the intervention of the local police who fired shots above the heads of the fighters, dispersing the Arabs who ran in every direction. The police then arrested all the crew members and locked them up, more for their own protection. The police then escorted them back in the motor launches to the ship.

At 21hours the ship left Aden for Port Fremantle, Western Australia. Heavy weather was forecast. While the crew closed the port hole dead lights, the saloon stewards secured all loose furniture, and the ship's tannoys warned passengers of the danger of going up on deck during the storm. At 0200 hours the storm hit the ship. Fortunately, most of the passengers were asleep in their cabins. The only reported injury was a middle aged man who fractured his elbow after falling down the stairway. Damage was slight — mostly crockery and a few panes of glass.

The storm soon passed and the following morning found the ship in pleasant weather. The water taken on at Aden was not agreeable with the children being Bor water. This caused concern with the parents because it was essential for all to drink plenty of water in the intense heat. A delegation of fathers approached the ship's doctor about the problem. He assured them the water was quite safe to drink and advised them to add cordial to the water to improve the taste. The Doctor then advised them to see the Chief Steward who immediately summoned the Second Stewards and Head Waiters demanding to know why cordial was not on the dining tables.

In the meantime some of the children's fathers took it upon themselves to go below to where the cordial was stored. They then issued cordial to all who wanted it. We the stewards were then told off for not having it on the tables. I for one did not know about placing cordial on the tables.

We did not do it on the U.S.A. run. This offering cordial was, we were told normal practice in the tropics, and it certainly did solve the problem.

The following morning the sea had calmed but it was very humid so the port holes were opened on the higher decks to let the air circulate.

The food on the *Georgic* was always of the highest standard, fresh every day. Food from the day before was put down the shoots on the stern of the ship. Flocks of sea birds made short of the scraps; the sight of an albatross was always welcome, providing it did not land on the ship. That was bad luck.

The menu in the saloons changed from day to day with a wide choice to suit all appetites. Early meals for children were available. The only thing that passengers needed money for was drinks at the bar and cigarettes. Alas, some of the emigrants wer so short of money it was a common thing to see them borrowing from the crew — especially the children.

The Big Brother Organisation were taking twelve lads from the Orphanages of Liverpool to Melbourne. They were usually well behaved; save for the frequent fisty cuffs between themselves, they had their own overseers, mostly school teachers, taking advantage of the half way round the world free cruise, and receive payment for doing it. Still, they did a good job. They also assisted in the one hour per day education of all children of age. St.Vincent de Paul Society, helped would-be emigrants who could not raise the ten pounds per head, and of course all ex-service men and their families went free.

Petty thieving was a problem both with passengers and some crew. The Masters of Arms had their work cut out. Then a said-to-be radio message was received from Liverpool Police back in England, they had good reason to believe the ship was carrying a fugitive amongst the passengers. The story went that a factory in Liverpool had been raided by two men wearing masks, armed with pick axe handles, the day before the ship set sail. One had made his escape to Ireland, the other was aboard ship with the £5000 wages of the factory workers.

A ship the size of *Georgic* with 1800 passengers and 500 crew, the men being segregated from the women, could quite easily harbour a criminal say for a week's voyage, but to be inconspicuous for a 4 week voyage would require an accomplice, some person who could go to all parts of the ship or talk to any person in the line of his duty without raising suspicion. Getting on board ship in Liverpool would not have been so difficult, with all the confusion with the stewards' walk off; no one bothered to count the number of stewards who walked off the ship, and certainly no one counted them when they went back on board.

Passenger lists were checked, but no person could be pinpointed. Then the Masters at Arms made a search of the ship but to no avail, they then embarked on a surprise search on the promenade deck at night, but were sent packing by the courting couples, and passengers escaping the heat of the cabins by sleeping on the cooler decks. They then seemed to give up the ghost, until a man was reported overboard and missing. It was soon found the whole thing was a hoax. However, one member of the crew was caught red-banded stealing from a cabin mate's locker. His punishment was to have his left hand put into an open port hole and while two hefty cooks held bim, a third slammed down the dead light onto his knuckles. Of course the officers knew nothing of this, and as he still had his right hand, he would have to carry out his duties. This served as a warning to any would-be thieves among the crew. On 3rd June we crossed the equator, that was a wonderful day when all the passengers received the Certificate of King Neptune and the more hardy took the 'Dip'. Parties were taking place all over the ship. It was my first time across the equator and so I was as excited as

Berth Card.

MRS. K. LAKE.

Ship

Cabin No. A70 / Berth No. C

Please have this card in your hand when you embark.

ACCOUNT OF WAGES

Name of Ship and Official Number	Description of Voyage or Employment	Reference Number in Agreement
M.V. "GEORGIC" 162,369	Government Service	2/291

Name of Seaman	Rating	Date of Engagement	Date of Discharge	Rate of Wages
J. Curly	Seaman	6·9·45	3·1·46	£13·10

EARNINGS	AMOUNT	DEDUCTIONS	AMOUNT
Wages @ £ ... per month for 4 months ... days.	62	Reduction of Wages on disrating by £ ... per month for ... months ... days	
Increase of wages on promotion by £ ... per month for ... months ... days	40	Income Tax Payable under Class ... H.1	8 16
War Risk		Union Fees	1 7
Total	102	Ins. 17 Weeks E.	
Deductions	98 15 2	Health and Pensions	16 2
	£ 3 4 10	Unemployment	
8 Days Leave Pool Pay	4 2 8	Cash	27 12 6
Subsistence	1 4	Superannuation	
	£ 8 11 6	Hospital	8 6
		Wine A/c.	
Less ... Days		Fines and Forfeitures	
Plus ... Days		Advance on Joining	
		Allotment	59 10
		Days Leave Taken	
		War Risk not due on Leave	
BALANCE DUE	8 11 6	TOTAL DEDUCTIONS	98 15 2

Dated at the Port of Liverpool

this 3 of Jan 19 46 .... (Signature of Master).

anybody. This did not mean we were off duty; it happened that all our diners decided on a buffet which was provided on deck and in the main lounge which enabled most of us stewards the chance to join the festivities. The celebrations went on until the early hours without incident, except for some boys, who had wandered down to the working alley, where to their delight they found the electric buggy, which a crew member had foolishly left the starting key in. After flattening the batteries by racing up and down, they dropped the key down the lift shaft.

The following day was uneventful save for the passing of a P.& 0. liner homeward bound.

I recall some of my passengers saying if they ever saw another ice cream again after landing, it would be too soon. I must admit, ice cream every day for the entire trip was a bit much, albeit every other day was chocolate flavoured. An Irish family totalling 16 wanted to change their port of entry from Melbourne to Fremantle, the father claiming he had been offered work in Perth whilst on the ship. Permission was refused on the grounds that special arrangements had been made in Melbourne to house such a large family.

From Fremantle to Sydney I would assist the steward on the adjoining tables. Mike was happy not to be losing the large Irish family who he had catered for since leaving Liverpool, especially two of the girls who washed and ironed his shirts.

Dinner was rather special that last night. My passengers dressed in their best. A large magnificent cake centred the tables, bearing the word FAREWELL; miniature flags of the Red Ensign alongside and Australia Ensign adorned the topping. The menu included Consomme Royale, Poached Fresh Salmon, Roast Beef or Lamb, Veg, Desserts, with 4 bottles of Australian wine per table. The Irish father whispered something in his son Brendon's ear, the lad responded by leaving the saloon

M.V. GEORGIC

CERTIFICATE OF KING NEPTUNE

This is to certify that *Josef H. Bott.*
has crossed the Equator in His Britannic Majesty's
M.V. Georgic, and has this day been duly initiated
as a Son/Daughter of Neptune in accordance with the
ancient rites and ceremonies which have existed
from time immemorial.

We do hereby proclaim him/her a free citizen of all
our seas.

We charge all our subjects, be they Mermen, Mermaids,
Sea-serpents, Dolphins, Whales, Sharks, Polliwogs or
whatnot, to refrain from eating, playing with or otherwise maltreating his/her person should the aforesaid
fall overboard.

Further, we enjoin all those whom it may concern to
deal with this our subject in all brotherly love, and to
extend the fin of friendship towards him/her whenever
possible.

Given under our Hand and Seal at our Court on the
Equator in Longitude 67° E this 26th day of January,
in the year 1950 A.D.

Neptunus Rex.

Charles J. Williams
CAPTAIN

M.V. "GEORGIC"
(Captain C. S. WILLIAMS)

Built by : Harland & Wolff Limited, Belfast
Date of building : 1932
Description of engine : Vertical reciprocating internal
combustion

Gross Tonnage	...	...	*27,408 tons*
Nett Tonnage	...	...	*15,402 tons*

Speed : 17½ knots

DISTANCES

	MILES
Liverpool (PIER HEAD) to Point Lynas	50
Point Lynas to Gibraltar	1,239
Gibraltar to Port Said	1,912
Port Said to Suez	85
Suez to Aden	1,806
Aden to Melbourne (PORT PHILLIP)	6,430
Melbourne to Sydney	530
Total distance	11,552

Left Liverpool 10 Jan. 1950 - - Arrived Melbourne 8 Feb. 1950

Passengers (including one child born at sea)					...	2,004
Crew ...	...	...	...	...	...	486
				Total souls on board		2,490

then returned carrying a bottle of Paddies Irish Whiskey, handing it to his father.

'Give everyone a shot will ye Steward, and give ye self one.'

I thanked the generous father and circled the two tables putting in a decent portion in the empty wine glasses after pouring myself a wee one. The half steamed father announced he would like to make a toast.

'God Bless the lot of you, it's been a pleasure to meet you, especially you, and ye mates, Steward and the Head Waiter.'

It was now apparent he'd had a good drink earlier. "That's enough now Dad,' pleaded young Brendon, 'Sit ye down before ye fall down'.

They all roared laughing while toasting each other. Breakfast was served early that morning, the date 8th June.My passengers had collected £15 between them all, be it a mixture of one white £5 note, 3 sterling £1 notes, 6 Irish punts and the rest made up of coins.

I thanked all and had bid them farewell. They had promised to write to me when they had settled. I was grateful for the £15, it was more than I expected. On the New York run one passsenger would tip £25, but then they were wealthy. Some stewards got nothing, not a penny, because of their arrogance towards their passengers. One steward who was tipsy most of the day everyday, would fill the water jug with gravy and plonk it in the middle of his table, telling the demoralized passengers to help themselves, then when serving the dessert, would give the same jug a quick rinse under the tap in the kitchen, and fill it full of custard. He was logged more than once, but persisted in his drunken manner.

Another steward would have at least two pint jugs of ale hidden under the dumb waiter and so reeked of ale as he floundered his way through the meals. The head waiters were aware of the goings on, but would turn a blind eye. Had they dismissed the offending stewards from the saloon, they could not replace them because of the shortage of stewards. The old time steward on the next tables to myself was tipped £25 in all, for he treated his passengers as he would on the *Coronia* doing a Round the World Cruise.

Shore leave was granted to the crew in Fremantle and I, being off duty until the ship sailed 1700hrs — the notice stated at the top of the gangway — made my way ashore with nine shipmates at 15. 10hrs. We were enjoying ourselves in the 'P.& O' Bar on the High Street when the bar tender enquired if we were from the *Georgic*. After telling him we were, he then advised us our ship was pulling away from her birth. We immediately scarpered down to the quayside to find she had gone. We all were sure the time of sailing was set at 17.00hrs. But here we were on the quayside at 15.30hrs. and she had gone.

The cargo/passenger ship *Gothic* was tied up in the next birth so we boarded her to seek advice. An officer of the *Gothic* advised us to go to the Seamen's Mission. This we did, to be advised to give ourselves up to the Local Police, as Seamen in Distress. The outcome was we were all charged for entering the country illegally and sentenced to 6 weeks imprisonment.

I being under eighteen was put on probation until a ship could be found to send me home. I never did see my shipmates again. But hearsay has it when the skipper heard of the imprisonment, requested that the men be allowed to join the ship at Melbourne. I after being well looked-after in a home in Perth for 4 weeks was found a position as pantry boy on the *Port Duneden* bound for Hull and home, and my boys' wage of £10.12s.6d. per month.

After the *Georgic* disembarked 40 emigrants at Fremantle, Western Australia she sailed to Melbourne where 1200 disembarked. Sixteen members of the crew missed the ship here and had to fly (at their own expense) to Sydney to await the ship. On arrival at Sydney the *Georgic* landed the remainder of the emigrants. The sixteen crew members had now arrived from Melbourne and were allowed to board the ship, all sixteen were logged.

One crew member was taken off the ship by the Australian Police to appear in court for wounding another crew member in a brawl while the ship was at sea; he received a prison sentence and after was deported back to England.

The *Georgic* left Sydney on June 23rd for Siegon where she took on 1500 French and Arab Legioners. The troops were a magnificent sight as they paraded on quayside. A hundred or more Arab Legioners mounted on pure white stallions flanked the foot soldiers. They were destined for Algiers where trouble was erupting. When all the troops were boarded, the *Georgic* set sail for Aden and Port Said.

The smell on board was overpowering, they may well have looked very smart on the quayside, but once on board, with their smelly desert boots, many attempts were made to get rid of the foul smell but to no avail.

Vino, being the Legioner's favourite drink, many thousands of gallons had been purchased in Saigon, and of course French food, garlic by the ton. Being limited to two bottles per day did not go down well with the tough Legioners, so it was not surprising when a black market was connived between the stewards in the saloons, who waited on the ever hungry and thirsty soldiers. The stewards were in the position of being allowed to purchase any amount of vino which they sold to the Legioners at exorbitant prices and if the Legioners ran out of money, they would part with wrist watches etc. to get their hands on the vino. Surprisingly there was no trouble reported through-out the voyage.

Nº 25921

COMMONWEALTH OF AUSTRALIA
DEPARTMENT OF IMMIGRATION
AUSTRALIA HOUSE
LONDON

21st September 19.49

Document of Identity

This Document is issued in lieu of a Passport to :

Herbert Ernest LOVE

for travel to Australia as an approved migrant accompanied by his
wife .... and .... children as speci
fied on the back hereof.

DESCRIPTION

BEARER   WIFE

NATIONALITY ...... BRITISH

Place of Birth............ Bournemouth Hants

Date of Birth 3/1/1922

Height   5' 9"

Colour of Eyes...... ....Blue

Colour of Hair. .... Dark Brown

Visible Distinguishing Marks. Scar on

left cheek

SPECIMEN SIGNATURE

[signature]
Chief Migration Officer.

*This document is valid for a single journey only and must be surrendered to
the Immigration Authorities at the Port of Disembarkation in Australia.*

Passing through the Suez Canal, she arrived at Port Said where she collided with the Motor Vessel *Langkoeas* receiving superficial damage to her bow. On arrival in Morocco the Legioners disembarked. The Captain ordered that every available man should be engaged in spraying the ship from top to bottom with disinfectant until the awful smell was gone.

She arrived back home in Liverpool on July 30th where she berthed, then had the damaged bow put right.

On August 23rd, 1955, after notifying all emigrants who had booked to sail on her — (the ship is not a luxury vessel), she sailed for Sydney. It had been decided to go via Capetown to avoid the tragic experiences on her last voyage through the Suez. Showering in cold water below decks is not a pleasant experience but both passengers and crew tolerated it. But this was compensated by a much improved and varied menu. From the outset of the voyage the stewards were disgruntled with pay and conditions and engaged in strikes which caused serious disruption in the running of the ship. Some jumped ship at Capetown, others were jailed for being drunk and disorderly.

Some of the crew had a running feud with members of the crew of *Himalaya* which only stopped with the intervention of the local police. Leaving Capetown, the *Georgic* ran into very heavy weather in the Indian Ocean which the Captain attempted to avoid by taking a course into the cold southern waters that made life unpleasant for several weeks. Then the ship started to waddle from side to side. This was clearly seen by standing on the aft deck and looking at the wake of the ship which never seemed straight. There was slight zigzag; whether this was caused by a damaged prop or not, nobody seemed to know. The old ship just ploughed her way through the mountainous seas onward towards Australia.

The Marconi International Marine Communication Co., Ltd.

Marconi House, Chelmsford

TO-DAY'S NEWS

S.S. G E O R G I C

Press message from the Wireless Station at O X F O R D ...... Date 6-11-49 ... Words 376 ...

LONDON.

Opposition intends demanding a Parliamentary debate on the report of the Overseas Food Commission issued today. Corporations report covering the East African Ground Nut scheme shows liabilities over 123 millions incurred and only £423,000 earned while Treasury auditors adversely commented on accounting methods.

LONDON.

Economic Cooperation Administration approved a project for machinery purchases for a Petroleum Chemical plant at Grangemouth, Scotland involving an outlay of nine million Dollars Marshall Aid funds. Products will be used in plastic and rayon industries, textile and manufacturing and drugs and dye stuffs.

RACING.

Result:- Workboy 80-1. Editor 5-1. Grassington 9-4 (Favourite). Nine ran.

Taunton. County Handicap steeplechase. Probables, betting:- 9-4 Dusky Chimes. 100-30 Xander. 6-1 Fair Drift. 8-1 Twins Chloe. 10-1 Fair Enough, Volauvent 2nd., 180-9 Longbow. 25-1 Killtern, Perchance to Dream, Tredilion, Murty, Allens Bridge, Laced Up.

LONDON.

Miss New Zealand (Mary Woodward of New Plymouth) was presented to the Queen at Victoria League meeting with representatives from Auckland, Canterbury, Marlborough, New Plymouth, Otago, Poverty Bay, Warrington and Wellington similarly honoured. Miss Woodward told Her Majesty all New Zealanders were hoping for a Royal visit to offset the cancellation of their previous tour and the Queen stated they still hope to make the visit.

FOOTBALL.

F.A. XI 4 Army 1. Charlton, Aston Villa 2 Sambrook Rovers 1.

Zurich. Germanys re-entry to International football confirmed and their first postwar match will probably be against Switzerland at Stuttgart during August.

AUCKLAND.

Approximately 800 waterside workers totalling half the unions strength were dismissed for refusal to work overtime with non-unionists and declining to replace dismissed men.

SYDNEY.

According to Trinidad importer Demonthrum the West Indies prepared to transfer Canadian and American trade formerly worth fifty million Dollars to Australia as devaluation prices bring West Indians reach.

SYDNEY.

Agricultural authorities estimate current New South Wales wheat harvest yielding up to 88 million bushels. Harvesting of early wheat is checked by Petrol shortages which may result in a loss of 18 million bushels.

SINGAPORE.

Court of Appeal ruled the Sultan of Johore not Sovereign ruler as his privileges waived by seeking Japanese court rulings during occupation.

—::::::::—

The *Georgic* arrived in Sydney on September 29th having first called at Fremantle and Melbourne. She arrived back in Liverpool on November 19th, 1955 a tired looking old lady.

Attempts were then made to sell her. The best offer received came from the Scrap Yard. Sadly the great ship sailed down the River Mersey from Liverpool to Kames Bay and the Tail of Banks where she was laid up. The date was 14th December, 1955.

―――――――――

Trish O'Donavan recalls . . .

With my parents and sister I arrived in Melbourne on the Queen's Birthday holiday Monday, June 13, 1955. We thought it must have been early closing day, as in England, because the shops were all closed. My parents first applied to migrate to Australia in 1948. Assisted passages were denied because my father's parents happened to be in America when he was born. After several refusals, my parents decided to lash out and we bought new beds, lounge suite and carpet squares (this was before fitted carpets became the norm. A few months later we received a letter informing us that "Passages have been booked for you on *M.V. Georgic* leaving Liverpool on Friday, May 13th, 1955." Assisted passages had been granted. I'm still very proud to say that I paid my own way to Australia― all £5 of it! The full adult rate was £10.

My parents had just 6 weeks to sell the car, an Austin Ruby which sold for £90 and the furniture. My uncle was given power of attorney to sell the house. During that six weeks I was invited to the homes of people I hardly knew — my friends' grandparents, my boy-friend's aunty, etc.

Everyone seemed to be even more excited about the family's emigration than we were. My work-mates presented me with an evening bag but said they doubted I'd have much use for it in a place where kangaroos hopped down the main street.

LIVERPOOL. Had my first, and only, view of the Liver Birds. Boarded M.V. *Georgic* Thursday, May 12. Accommodation was in cabins with 8-10 bunks. Mothers and children shared cabins and the fathers were in other, near-by carbins.

M.V. Georgic was a floating city with hairdressers, barbers, coffee shops, hospital, etc. Every evening, various forms of entertainment were provided— recent films, concerts by professionals and some very good amateurs, dances, games, etc.

The winner of a series of talent quests was an 84 year old man who had to be commended for his sheer doggedness. His prize, awarded by the Captain, was a cigarette-case with an engraving of M.V. *Georgic* on its lid. We were all delighted for him and shared his disappointment when it was stolen.

The ship was short of crew members and took on anyone who was willing to sail. Unfortunately, a full crew was not obtained and passengers were encouraged to work as dish-washers for a wage of about 10/- per shift. This was more than the crew members were paid and led to unrest among both the regular sailors and the Johnny-come-latelys. On one occasion, a non-regular decided he would join a family for lunch. I suspect he had his eyes on the teenage daughter who was told by the dining room steward that crew members were not allowed in the passengers' dining room.

She said, "I didn't invite him."

A steward with a tray of full plates dropped the lot on the floor! The ship's doctor, a big, burly man arrived and proceeded to knock the troublemakers senseless. Because of the sailors' superstition about leaving port on a Friday 13th, cast-off was delayed until Saturday 14th. At the 1pm sitting for lunch, our steward was a likeable 19-year old Liverpudlian named Eddie. During lunch, he told us that until 12 o'clock that day he had been working in a factory. He had signed on in order to escape the compulsory National Service.

After lunch, he said, "See you on Monday!"

We thought there would be no food served on Sunday but he said we'd all be sea-sick. He was wrong! At breakfast on Sunday, he looked very green-faced and we didn't see him for a couple of days.

The food served on board was of such a high standard that we just longed for plain old bread and jam! But we did wonder about the ladies who turned up for breakfast with their hair in rollers.

M.V. *Georgic* had been a troop-carrier during the war. When we boarded we were very aware that the ship had been freshly painted. Everything was sparkling. Not so after a couple of weeks at sea! There were cigarette burns and other damage all over the place. At the end of the voyage, the hundreds of brand-new deck-chairs had been· torn to shreds and the lounge suites were in tatters. The damage was not of the kind caused by children so we wondered just what type of person was being allowed to emigrate to Australia. The Bay of Biscay was very rough and it disgusted us to see adults vomiting in the corridors. The ship's crew did wonders with the cleaning up.

I can remember only two of the passengers who earned themselves nicknames. 'Tojo' was a large man with a black moustache. He seemed to argue about all the official decisions that were made — probably became mayor of the town in which he settled. The other was 'Tex'.

I think he was Australian. He entertained children, young and old, with his 'bush bass' and his singing. The "bush bass' was made from a tea chest, a broom-stick and some thin rope. By altering the angle at which the broom-stick rested on the tea-chest, and pulling the rope which joined the two, he was able to produce double-bass-like sounds. Some people referred to him as the 'loud-mouthed Aussie' but I think he was just using his talents to entertain others.

After a few days at sea, we reached the semi tropics and the skies clouded over. Each morning at breakfast the ship's doctor would broadcast on the radio and beg people to keep their toddlers' delicate skin covered. He warned, over and over, that grey days were burning days. Many people ignored his words. Suddenly, we missed seeing a few toddlers on deck with Mum and Dad. They appeared a few days later swathed in bandages. Two babies died on the voyage and we saw, very early in the morning, their burials at sea. Impetigo was rife but this wasn't necessarily from uncleanliness because the warmer climate encourages growth of all sorts of germs.

When we reached the port of Aden we were met by dozens of bum-boats laden with baskets and all sorts of souvenir-like junk. The idea was that you bargained for an article, caught the basket-on-a-rope thrown by the trader and let it down to the bum-boat where the article you wanted was placed in it. You then hauled up the basket containing the article, put your money in the basket and let the basket down to the trader. We knew of many passengers who willingly cheated the traders.

The sun in Aden was unbelievably hot and I wore my Dad's long-sleeved shirt to protect my arms. The air was very clear and dry because the last time rain had fallen was 19 years before. We hired a taxi and a very pleasant driver. He drove us to a hotel which had lots of 'Certificates of Hygiene and Cleanliness' on the walls. I had a lime milk-shake. During our tour of Aden I can remember seeing a very pregnant woman on her hands and knees sweeping the road with a little bundle of sticks. I can also remember seeing a man with elephantiasis, something I'd only ever seen in my school biology book.

Back on board, from the ship's rail, we saw our likeable Liverpudlian steward being chased by the land-police. He jumped into a speed-boat, picked up and tossed overboard the two legal occupants and made his way back toward the ship. He jumped from the boat and swam a short distance till he reached the ship. The boat was last seen going round and round in circles.

I had intended to train as a teacher so I was very pleased to be able to help out in the ship's school. Unfortunately, I lost my very good pen there— or was it lifted — as was a watch which was a going-away present from my Grandmother?

(I gave up teaching kids 4 years ago and am now involved in teaching Adult Literacy (paid!) and working for Kip McGrath, tutoring children who have problems at school).

When we reached the port of Fremantle we were taken on a bus tour of the city. We saw lots of school-children at play in the school yards and were very surprised to see how tanned they were. It wasn't until many years later that I realised they were probably only slightly less new to the country than I was and possibly didn't have a very good command of the English language. It was very interesting to watch streams of people heading for the shopping centre. We knew what they were after — we bought fish and chips, too!

One of the Australian padres on the ship made every effort to entertain groups of people to morning or afternoon tea in his cabin. He somehow managed to squeeze ten or twelve cups of tea from his tiny tea-pot. I believe he entertained every family on board. He made us feel already welcome to his country.

A few months before we left England, we had seen a T.V. programme in which the life of this Minister had been featured. He had first arrived in Australia on a sailing ship with his parents.

There were 1800 passengers on board M..V. *Georgic* and of these, 1200 disembarked at Melbourne. Those destined for Adelaide were taken by what friends described as cattle trucks. We left the ship at Melbourne. Friends who went to Sydney told us that the rest of the voyage was very eventful. Some crew members went on strike and passengers were again encouraged to do their work, but at a higher rate of pay. This caused 'gang-warfare' resulting in one person's death.

When the ship reached Brisbane, I believe some crew-members gate-crashed a dance being held by The Irish Foresters, (possibly a Lodge). The Police were called and the crew-members were jailed.

The 'Georgic' at Station Pier, Melbourne

On arrival in Melbourne we were taken to a reception centre situated behind the Exhibition Buildings. We were taken on tours of the city and after due 'processing" we were taken to the Commonwealth Hostel in Preston. There we were issued with blankets, some of them crawling with moth maggots.

Accommodation was in Nissan huts and each morning at 6 o'clock we would be wakened by our next door neighbours alarm clock. Food at the Hostel was plain but plentiful and nourishing. Each evening we wrote on a paper bag what type of sandwiches we wanted for lunch the next day. After breakfast we picked up our named bags and went off to work and school. The Manageress of the hostel was a very assertive lady of European origin. She was generally known as Irma Grise, after the concentration camp superintendent. Sandwich lunches were a bit hard to get used to after our two-course hot lunches in England.

In England, my sister· had won a scholarship to Grammar School. In Victoria, she was put into Grade 8 at the local parish primary school. It was no wonder that she felt short-changed, played truant and threw away her sandwich lunches.

My father had a job to come to in Melbourne and started pretty-well straight away. I was granted a studentship i.e. the sum of £20.17s.2d. per fortnight in payment and a two-year course of training in primary teaching, for which I was under bond to work for the Education Department for a minimum period of two years. The course started on June 29. Two weeks into my course at Melbourne Teachers College the Principal sent for me and told me that I was to be put into a College hostel because conditions in a Commonwealth hostel are not conducive to study. The College hostel was a lovely old mansion in South Yarra.

My fellow-residents were country girls, mainly

from Gippsland in the eastern part of Victoria, and I spent weekends at many of their homes. I also found myself a country boyfriend whose parents welcomed me into their home. The romance wore a bit thin when his parents took me out on a surprise trip - to the SNOW!! They thought I'd love it but I nearly froze to death and had no desire to ever see snow again until some twenty years later.

My fellow-students all seemed to be very proficient at dressmaking and other needlecrafts. Their mothers were marvellous scone and pavlova-makers and morning or afternoon teas, even if only a cuppa and biscuits, were always served on fine china and lace or hand embroidered tablecloths. Even the poorest of households knew how to play host beautifully. At the time, I noticed that some people were 'anti-Pom' and when I mentioned that I too was a Pom, they'd say, 'Oh, but you're different. We know you.' I heard this many times. It seems that people were afraid of the immigration programme because they feared it would mean loss of jobs for Australians.

All my friends were of Anglo-Saxon descent and they were shocked to the core when I asked if they were of convict descent. I soon learned not to ask such an insulting question. Nowadays, convict ancestry is something to be proud of!. One of the first books I tried to buy in Melbourne was a book of Australian folk songs. Impossible! There was no such book in print.

My fellow-student teachers knew the British folk songs but I knew more Australian folk songs than they did.

Meanwhile, my parents had left the Commonwealth hostel and were living in a one roomed sleep-out behind the house of one of my mother's workmates. I think they regretted leaving the hostel long before the suggested two-year residency. It was thought that migrants could begin to establish themselves after that two year period. They moved into an almost completed house in East Ringwood. The owner-builder had tried to commit suicide after his marriage broke up and the cheap rent was in return for cooking and doing his washing and cleaning. That lovely house seemed to be at the ends of the earth — just 25 kilometres from the heart of Melbourne in bushland which no longer exists. The house didn't have a laundry so Mum had to get out in the back yard and light a wood fire under a copper boiler. This, after having been used to a semi-automatic washing machine, was very hard on Mum. I was offered a block of land in Ringwood East for £25 but on my fortnightly allowance of £20.17.2d, less deduction for board, I couldn't afford it.

Mum and Dad and my sister then moved to a 2-bedroomed house in Blackburn. They still didn't have enough money to buy a house, so Dad took a job at the Woomera rocket range in South Australia. He wasn't a very big man but he lost a lot of weight and gained a sun-tan as he pushed around barrow-loads of sand. Years later he died of cancer and I still wonder whether he had been exposed to fall-out.

After my initial teacher-training I chose to teach in the country, mainly in 2-teacher schools with about 35 pupils. My mother was very concerned that I'd have no social life but that wasn't the case at all. In the bush, life was a ball but I did have to watch my 'decorum'. At that time, it was a bit disconcerting to have a little group of 4-7 year. olds chanting, "We know your boyfriend."

My parents had applied for a Commission House. They received a letter stating, that unless I lived at home with them, they were ineligible for Government housing. my Principal took, me to visit the local M.P. He said he was having lunch with the Housing Minister and that he would tell him how very important it was to have young teachers in the Bush. About 3 weeks later, my parents were granted a Commission house.

Having saved up and bought a car, I was able to get board in nearby town. There I met my future husband, a city boy visiting his sister. Six weeks after we met we agreed to marry and I'm very proud to tell anyone that I lived with my first husband. My husband's mother's family came to Australia in about 1830. He grew up with Australian born/Anglo-Saxon/Celtic friends. Our four grown-up children have friends of many ethnic backgrounds.

Our children and nieces and nephews have married partners of varied extractions — German, Italian, American, Irish, Chinese and a few Aussies for good measure. This exercise really made me think! The English vocab. was, still is, very different. In College, there were many references to 'Coles', 'Clag', and 'Durex'. Coles is a store similar to Woolworths, Clag is a starch paste and Durex wasn't a condom brand but a brand of sticky tape.

My mother didn't settle into life in Australia for quite a few years. Nothing seemed to suit her. Even the g-um-trees weren't a real 'tree-green' . When her father became very ill, she flew 'home' to be with him. She then wrote to tell us that she couldn't wait to be home in Australia again. That was about thirty-five years ago.

Mum has since made several trips back to England and is now an Australian Citizen. I can't help but admire my parents for the courage they had in deciding to leave a comfortable life in England in order to build a better life for themselves and their children here, in Australia.

Mr. George and Lilian Simpson of Dunsborough, West Australia when asked if they arrived in Australia aboard the *Georgic* said ...

"Yes, we was on the *Georgic* sailed on the 14 May 1955, should have been the 13th, but the crew went on strike as we got on board. Our boat train from London hit a vehicle and we was kept on the train for hours. We had five children under twelve years of age. Women's Voluntary Service eventually helped us but what a send off from Mother England, — Friday 13th did — I thought it was the end, 'cause I am and always have been a worrier. Had a bit of a rough trip round Spain, but into the Mediterranean it was beautiful - it got hot.

The Arabs at Port Said calling us Scotch wogs and selling their wares, people cheating them with taking things and not paying, then on to Aden — it was hot, having never leaving the coast of England before.

I must say whoever was in charge done a very good job looking after us all, keeping the children cool "with heat rash". We was told the *Georgic* was sunk in Suez during the war, she was a big ship, the inner metal plates were badly buckled.

Our two Scottish ladies at sea aboard the 'Georgic', October 1949

Charlie Lynch snapping one on board 'Georgic', October 1949

Mr Punter from Medina, Western Australia 6167 states -

"My wife and I and three children arrived in Fremantle aboard the *Georgic* in June 1955, after what was a rather trying voyage from Liverpool.

I don't think the vessel was equipped to take so many people as there were only enough seats on deck for about half so those that had 2nd sitting (us) only got a seat while the 1st sitting were having their meals. We spent most of the day hanging over the rail.

The weather in the Red Sea was far too hot and it was almost impossible to get a cold drink; on one occasion

I queued up for 2 hours only to have the bar shut as I reached it.

━━━━━━━━━━━━━━

John Ellis of Somerville, Victoria, Australia, he wrote ...

"I was instructed by the emigration people at Australia House, London, to embark on the liner *Georgic* which was berthed at the Landing Stage, Liverpool on the 10th January, 1949.

I travelled by train from Doncaster, changing at Sheffield and Manchester, after going through the official formality before boarding the vessel and enjoying my first meal on board which was lunch.

I had to share a cabin with three other young men. The cabin was the last one aft on the starboard side on 'D' deck. We were not allowed ashore again until we reached Australia. But we were looked after quite well.

The food was very good. Supplied by the Australian Government, food which the people of England had never seen for years.

The full passenger list was 2,020 and 750 of that was children. We were told that at that time, this was the largest number of people to move from one country to another. The last statement I doubt, as the *Queen Mary* moved nearly 16,000 troops etc. during the war on one voyage.

Margaret Stephenson sailed on the *Georgic* on the same voyage as myself and was certainly misinformed when she was told the crew went on strike because the ship was going to sail on Friday 13th.

She continued "We were not allowed to go back ashore so had to go to the galley to get our own evening meal which was chaotic. Mothers trying to pacify screaming babies was the worst sight, as they tried to get warm milk for them. My most vivid memories are of the buckled corridors due to the wartime bombing. The wonderful smooth voyage. The terrible heat as we had no air conditioning. I shared a cabin at the bottom of the ship with eight other women, my top bunk was directly under a huge hot water pipe about 18" above my body. We arrived in Melbourne on 13th June 1955 which was a public holiday for the Queen's Birthday. To us it was a perfect summer's day though the locals were wearing jumpers and complaining of the winter."

In 1946, the *Georgic*, homeward bound to Liverpool, experienced trouble between civilian and service women over accommodation. This led to the cessation of civilians on troop ships unless in emergency.

John Alton of Moreton, Lancashire, who lost a hand in a grenade explosion whilst serving in the RAF, and who was totally blinded by another hand grenade in India in 1944, sailed aboard the *Georgic* on the ship's first emigrant run to Australia. He was given a special permit at the direction of the Australian Minister of Immigration, having taken a two year course at a special training school for the blind, enabling him to get a position in the Air Line Industry. His wife and two daughters accompanied him. Alas, the voyage was delayed when the port side prop was fouled by a rope and the ship had to re-dock. A search was carried out by the Master of Arms when reports were made of stowaways on board. Having inspected every likely place, including of course the life boats, none were to be found.

However, on arrival in Australia, two young men gave themselves up to Immigration Officers and were arrested. They both received six weeks in jail for illegally entering the country. Whilst serving their sentences, a check was made on their background back in England. They were found to be of good character and simply had not been bothered with the normal procedure of immigration.

After serving their sentence, they were allowed to stay, first paying their ten pound fare to the Cunard White Star.

The 'Georgic' approaching Sydney

From Richard Southey's Diary

Friday 7th October 1949.
Set off for Australia, lovely morning, train full, platform packed with people in high spirits. Left London 8.45pm for Liverpool.

Saturday 8th October
Margaret and Derek not too grand, everything else O.K
2 o'clock last sight of England (Bishop's Lighthouse).
Entered Bay at Midnight. Played Housey Housey

Sunday 11th October
Sea pretty rough. Margaret not the best. Went to Church.

Monday 12th October
Reached Gibralter. Midnight - all on deck.

Saturday 17th October
Reached Port Said. Boats all around ship selling goods,
mostly leather. Young Arab caused fun doing tricks with
chickens. Margaret bought handbag and shopping bag.

Sunday 18th October
When we got up we were standing in Suez Canal waiting
for a convoy to pass. Saw an Arab riding his donkey while
his wife walked behind carrying a pitcher on her head.
Carried on through Suez. Seeing Arab villages, British
Colonies until we stopped in Second Lake.

Monday 19th October
Arrived at Aden, shore leave granted. Small boats sur-
rounded the ship selling table cloths, carpets and lots of
pretty goods. Margaret started her new bome by buying
2 carpets £4.0.0. 11 o'clock we are off again.

31st October
Seen nothing else but water. Everyone eager to land.

3rd November
10.00am we saw Australia for the first time.

The Fancy Dress Competition

The Children's Xmas Party Menu read like this . . .

Children's Xmas Party
held on board
M.V. 'GEORGIC"
Sunday, December 24 1950
In the Main Lounge

Hickory, Dickory Dock,
We start at 3.30 o'clock

Welcome chldren one and all,
The thin, the fat, the short, the tall:
Balloons and hats you here do see
To fill your little hearts with glee.

The Queen of Hearts, she made tarts
Cakes and pastries too
The Knave he stole them right away,
Now don't let that happen to you.

So eat and drink as much as you can,
Drink juice and milk too,
And let the "Georgic" party be
A happy Christmas at sea for you.

Menu
Orange Juice   Apple Juice
(Bells of St. Clements)

Assorted Fancy Pastries
(Alice in Wonderland)

Plum and Fruit Cake
(Little Jack Horner)

Jelly Creams

Bread and Butter
(Little Tommy Tucker)

Vanilla Ice Cream and Wafers
(Snow White)

Milk   Tea
Fresh Fruit

The Derman Family

A PENPAL BRIDE
by Mary A Tomlin

As a result of an advertisement in the Weekly Times, I became a penpal bride. My husband was an avid reader of the farmers' paper. We wrote to one another for a year before he popped the big question: "Will you marry me?" The answer was yes, but with a reservation that should we not like one another when we met we would not go ahead with the plans to marry.

George sent the money and I bought my engagement ring in Dundee, Scotland, and we were officially engaged on the 2nd April 1949. On the 13th September my twin brother and I celebrated our 21st birthday and that day I also received word that I had passed my medical and was now on the list awaiting a berth on a migrant ship to Australia. I didn't have long to wait as it was only two weeks later that I received notification that I was to sail on the M.V. *Georgic,* from Liverpool on the 7th October.

There was great excigement at home as I was the first to flee the nest and as we had no relatives or friends in Australia it was a very worried mother who bade her eldest daughter farewell, with the rest of the family at the station at Dundee, to travel with another migrant family to the Liverpool station. My twin brother was very upset as we were very close and had never been separated before. I waved goodbye to them all except Dad who travelled to Edinburgh with me where I had to change trains. I was on the first stage of my journey and it was with great trepidation that I waved my father goodbye. I was entirely on my own from now on as I embarked on my big adventure.

October 7th dawned wet and dreary and at 6pm we sailed from England's shores to the strains of the crowds on the wharf singing 'Will ye no' come back again.'

Fortunately for me I was a very good sailor and never missed a meal but felt very sorry for the people who were seasick. It took us a few days to find our sea legs and I have a good laugh when I recall the antics of us trying to climb up and down the stairs, especially when we got the tail end of a storm in the Bay of Biscay.

I soon made new friends and it wasn't long before the life on board ship was like one big happy family with organised games, dances, pictures etc. every day and night. The journey was quite smooth with only two stops on the way, at Port Said, and Aden. We were allowed ashore at Aden for a few hours which was very entertaining, as there was lots of bargaining between the migrants and the shopkeepers. We docked at Station Pier in Melbourne on the 7th November 1949 and it was the funniest feeling trying to walk on land again.

My fiance came on board to meet me and presented me with an opal and gold filligree broach which was beautiful.

When we left the ship we met his mother and his aunt on the quayside. We were to travel to Moonee Ponds by taxi, but as I hadn't been on an electric train before my request to go by train was accepted and it was rather funny trying to understand one another as I had a broad Scottish accent and I thought the Australians had a very funny accent. That night we toured the town of Melbourne and it was lovely to see all the bright lights after the very drab and dreary England where all the lights hadn't been turned on as yet after the war.

I was amazed at the shops being full of all sorts of goods as everything was still rationed in Britain.

We stayed in Melbourne for a few days and then set off on the train journey to Cobram. The names of some of the stations were of great amusement to me and I couldn't even pronounce them. We stopped at Seymour for something to eat and I was terrified in case the train would go without us. The same happened at Shepparton but I was too excited to eat.

We arrived at Strathmerton and my first impression was that I must be in the wilds somewhere, I wasn't prepared for the miles of roads, which were rough and full of potholes. The homes also seemed to be far apart and having been brought up in a city, I wondered what I had let myself in for. I had been used to all mod cons and it took a little bit of getting used to visiting the little house a mile down the back!!! Carting water from the dairy for washing and worst of all NO ELECTRICITY. How was I going to manage? It's amazing what one can do when one has to.

I stayed with neighbours, Mr & Mrs Hec Cathery, who had to nominate me as I had to go to a married couple's home before I married. They were very friendly and did all they could to make me feel at home. As George and I got along very well together we felt we could go ahead with our plans for the wedding.

As the house was ready to move into there was no need

for any delay and we were married within a month of me arriving in Australia.

As George's relatives all lived in and around Morwell, we decided to be married in Gippsland. We were married in the C of E church in a little village called Yinnar. George's sister Hilda and her husband Cyril made all the arrangements and Cyril gave me away. We had our honeymoon at Lakes Entrance and Traralgon. I didn't have time to be homesick as there were so many things to do settling into our nice new soldier settlement home and getting acquainted with the neighbours who were all very helpful to this new arrival from the old country.

Within our first year we had our first baby, a lovely little daughter weighing in at 5lbs 13ozs. followed 14$\frac{1}{2}$ months later by another girl 6lbs 4ozs. Their names— Mary Elizabeth the first born, named after her two grandmothers and Judith Margaret, a name George liked. They were very easy children to bring up and I was indeed fortunate not to have any problems with them.

It was a trial for me at first, doing the shopping in Cobram as I wasn't used to doing shopping for a family and also doing it in bulk. My accent caused a few problems at first.

The best part I enjoyed was the fact that I could go into a shop and buy what I wanted without having to produce any coupons, as there was no worry about rations. I had a very sweet tooth and my delight was to buy sweets without having to ration myself, as at home we were only allowed $\frac{1}{2}$ lb per month. I had many humorous experiences in the first few years in the shops trying to make myself understood, although I suspect the reason I was asked to repeat some of my requests was to hear my Scottish burr!!!

I joined the C.W.A. and R.S.L. Ladies Aux.'s and held a position of secretary in both of the organisations which I thoroughly enjoyed. We had lots to do and from a very raw migrant I soon learnt the ways of my new life. I made many friends amongst the settlers and their wives at Yarroweyah and will never forget my welcome and the way in which I was accepted as one of them.

━━━━━━━━

AN ASPECT OF THE AREA NOW KNOWN AS COBRAM SHIRE
by Mary Edwards

There were few made roads, no electricity and only the party line telephone connected to a few of the homes. In the dim dark ages? No!! Only 30 years ago on the Yarroweyah Soldier's Settlement.

As an immigrant, newly arrived from Scotland and married to my pen-friend, I settled down to an entirely new life — so different to the city life of a war torn nation, with everything from food to clothing still rationed. It was a delight to visit the shops and not have to worry about producing coupons for this or that.

Instead of living in a flat in a tenement I now, with my late husband—George Tomlin, had a lovely three bedroomed home with verandahs on the north, south and west sides of the house. The roads weren't named in those days, our address was Block 5. We had a wood stove in the kitchen, a copper in the laundry and a chip heater in the bathroom. With no electricity — the wood heap was a necessity, and we had to be careful with our water supply. The biggest change I had to overcome was the use of the 'little house', after having been used to sewerage all my life. This was a really backward step to me.

At first we had a dozen cows which George milked by hand and there was great excitement when the dairy was built and a petrol engine installed, followed at a later date by electricity, when all we had to do was press the button.

At the dairy there were six bails; at first we milked three cows at a time and eventually we doubled up the milking machines, enabling us to milk six cows at a time. In the early days cream was sent to Holdenson & Neilson at Numurkah three times a week. The truck picked up the cream and it also brought our ice for the ice chest we used in our kitchen. We had to be careful and remember to empty the water from the tray under the ice chest every night, otherwise there would be a flooded kitchen floor in the morning. At a later date most farmers changed to milk suppliers; first of all daily pickup of the milk cans and eventually the changeover to bulk refrigeration.

The milk was sent to Kraft at Strathmerton, and when the Murray Valley Dairy Company (Murray Goulburn) Factory was established, many of the Yarroweyah settlers were the first suppliers. We were one of the first fifty shareholders of the Murray Valley factory. We took out one hundred one pound worth of shares. I sold these in the early 1960s when I left Cobram to live in Finley.

The rabbits were in plague proportion in the early 1950s but with the advent of Myxomatosis, it wasn't long before the rabbits disappeared. Our eastern boundary fence adjoining Leighton Keast's property, had a sandhill which was riddled with rabbit warrens and it was a great advantage to both properties when Leighton cultivated the hill and installed spray irrigation. It was a beautful sight to see the lush green Lucerne growing instead of rabbits playing hide and seek. The excess Lucerne, when bailed, was sold. There was a mill at Katunga, Kimpton's, who as well as buying Lucerne also sold calf pellets and fodder for the chickens.

There were many trips to Numurkah, where the Soldier Settlement offices and depots were. We were able to purchase fence posts, droppers and wire. Contractors employed by the S.S.C. graded our land and helped put in the delvers. The settlers were supplied with a machinery shed and hay shed. The settlers were able to purchase their farms eventually, the values were as at 1948. Our farm was valued at £5,000 — quite different from today's values.

When the weather was bad, the rain made our roads very slippery and boggy. We were fortunate to have three different routes, and as a last resort, the Goulds of "Seven Hills" allowed us to use their drive through their property, which had an entry into their property in what is now called Blamey Road, and out the other side on the Katamatite — Cobram Road. Outside Allen Dougherty's was very bad and Allen and his boys were kept busy with their tractor pulling out cars after any heavy rain.

The Yarroweyah Hall was a very busy meeting place for the settlers, their wives and families. We had a very active C.W.A. and R.S.L. Ladies' Auxillary. I held the position of Secretary in both organisations. The year I was secretary of C.W.A. we held our Group Conference at the Yarroweyah Hall. It was a great success and I wrote the proceedings out in full for the "Cobram Courier" Mrs Bouchier was President and Mrs E. Babington was Group Secretary.

We also held a very successful C.W.A. Ball which was featured in the 'Weekly Times'. Mrs Jen Winter was president, Miss Nell O'Brien was treasurer, and myself secretary. Our branch of the C.W.A. also entered the Drama Festival held at Numurkah. We had a singing quartet and a play entered and were thrilled to win a prize and receive a bell suitably inscribed. It was used to call our meetings to order and held pride of place on our table at the meetings.

Even though we were all very busy on the farms, we still made time to hold dances, children's fancy dress balls, Euchre parties, etc. C.W.A. had a session on 3 SR run by Mrs Gronk. I wrote, on two consecutive years, a 12 minute essay — one being "A Penpal Bride" *(see previous article)* and the other 'A Tour of Scotland' and had the privilege of reading them on air.

My first Euchre party was quite a surprise as I had no idea what Euchre was. I soon learned and at the same time, when asked to bring a plate, DON'T bring it empty! There was no T.V. in those days and our entertainment kept us from being bored. There was always plenty to do and if you didn't feel inclined to go out, the radio and record player at home was always on the go.

Yarroweyah consisted of 1 store, 1 hall, 1 railway station. The store was run by Mr & Mrs Mudge followed by the Rossboroughs who also had a delivery service. The hall was put to good use as I have already mentioned. It was used as a Guide Hall and for the Scouts — who eventually got their own hall. Mrs Kit Hyde was on duty at the railway station which also housed the Post Office.

Our neighbours were the Leighton Keasts, last heard of they had moved to Tyabb. Gerry Shannon is now of Tatura, Allen Dougherty is now of Shepparton, Walkers had moved north but went back to Kyabram, Maudie and the late Hen Cathery, (Maudie has just moved to Deception Bay (Qld.)), where she has bought a nice home. Dulcie and the late Ken Heppell, Dulcie now lives in Shepparton.

The Matt Douthwaites went to Katamatite and there was also Frank Read and Keith James, the Water Bailiff. One of the first settlers to move were the Geoff Murphs who I believe live in Avoca. Most of the farms have changed hands now and many of the settlers are retired and living in Cobram. Bob and Muriel Hosie, Harry and Mrs Fox, Bob (who died recently) and Rita Ashcroft, Norm and Mrs Koch, Lex and the late Ted Duvall, just to name a few.

The first Scotsmen I met when I arrived were the late 'Scottie' Learmonth, Bob Christie and Bob Hosie who all made me feel welcome and at home. As my mother lives in Cobram I quite often meet my former neighbours. The Keith Melliers bought extra land and built a new home and have remained on the settlememt, they were our next door neighbours.

In 1957 I formed the Scottish Club known as The Heather Club. Kath and Jim Gardner, Mrs M. Wallace and Jean, Mary Clark, T. Breewel, Jim Gemmill, Bernie

Goodwin, Bob O'Hanlon, Wally Bowen and Mr Nicholls attended the first meeting. Many exciting times were had at the very popular dances which were held fortnightly.

1959 was a year of highlights when the first Highland Debutante Ball was held on 17th July. It was a big night, 50-50 dancing, modern dancing to the Black & White Orchestra from Nathalia at the cost of £21.10.0 and the Scottish dancing to the tune of Jimmy Shand records. 3SR broadcast the Ball at the cost of £24 and the four debs and their partners were presented to Mr George Moss; the Pipe Band was also in attendance. Nicky Hetreliz was the caterer and profits went to the Cobram Fire Brigade.

Mrs McGifford was the chaperone for the debs and Miss Young taught the girls and partners their presentation dance. Earlier in the year a very successful Burns Night was held on 22nd January 1959 — Nicky did the catering and the Haggis was made in Melbourne and sent to us at the cost of £3.19.2d. A Hallowe'en Night was held on 24th Oxtober 1959 when everyone dressed for the occasion.

———————————————

The following article entitled **'A Place in the Sun'** *and featured in a local newspaper was written by Wayne Gregson in 1987 . . . .*

A STRANGE letter arrived at the office yesterday.

It made those who read it proud, humble and ashamed to be Australian, all at the same time, and perhaps it's timely now that migration is in the news again.

It was from John Simpson, here it is, without any editing.

"Sir — 1955 was a good year for Poms. I, for one, arrived here to swell the ranks of migrants in the workforce; cannon fodder in the war of words that most Poms found themselves embroiled in.

"Part of the Dinkum Aussie delight in those days was slinging off at Poms, mainly to gauge their reactions.

"We were an unusual breed. Those of us who survived the verbal onslaught are still here, and very happy, thank you.

"My wife and I palled up on the MV *Georgic* during our migration in August 1955. Two lonely souls heading for a new life in a new country, not knowing what to expect. We married in December that same year, and during the next 31 years have increased the population by six, who, in turn have given us great joy and four grandchildren.

"My wife and I, being outnumbered six to two, and democratic to boot, also became Australian citizens. If you can't beat 'em, then join 'em.

"I am, nevertheless, proud to have taken the step.

"It would be very interesting to know how many from the MV *Georgic* of August 1955 are still here.

"We would like to know how many survived the initial two years that we 10-pound wonders were committed to. Who survived the early stigma of 'whinging Pom' which was quite prevalent then?

"In 1955 we Poms came with great dreams of fame and fortune. Some of us, let's say the majority of us, 31 years later have found what we came for, through hard work, diligence, and acceptance of what this great country has to offer.

"Some have probably found it earlier, I hope.

"Those that only whinged and did nothing hopefully have returned.

"The MV *Georgic*, dreadful tub of a ship that it was, is but a dim memory now. It went to the breakers' yard after our trip. Some of us thought it should have gone two trips earlier! The *Georgic* was a former troop carrier sunk in the Suez, and then re-floated for only three migrant trips around the Horn).

"To the expatriates, like the missus and I, who have

made it here, I ask: are you not glad you came and stayed?

"I, for one, wouldn't live anywhere else in the world right now. Things are getting too exciting to even contemplate a move. I've seen nothing of this great country yet.

"I also derive great pleasure in watching my young Aussies grow up in a country that so many people seem to want to continually label non-progressive and backward.

"Not a bit of it!

If the next 31 years are going to be anything like the last 31, this country is going to be a force to be reckoned with.

"And I am bloody glad I paid 10 pounds in 1955 to come out here to see it happen."

It was signed: John Simpson (ext Pom), Mt Waterley.

APITS found John Simpson, 55, at work yesterday, running his typesetting business, Just Type, in Cecil Place, Prahran.

"National pride needs a kick in the bum now," he said.

"There are too many who give up too easily, as a lot of those 10-pound Poms gave up too easily and went back home.

"I was like that for years until I woke up to myself and started giving as good as I got and made some life-long friends."

John, from Marlow in Buckinghamshire, his wife Edna, from Sittingbourne in Kent, and one son have run the typesetting business for the past 2½ years. The firm employs five people.

He said it made him sad to think of those who quit in the face of "dinkum Aussie" invective. He wonders how many potentially great Australians were forced to flee the country.

We, John, are bloody glad you came.

*AND yet another article found in the Melbourne Sun-Herald
in September 1995, and written by Sue Quinn in London read
as follows . . .*

THOUSANDS of former child migrants forced to emigrate
from Britain to Australia to help "seed the Empire" have
been offered fresh hope of reuniting with their families.

The Australian Child Migrant Foundation was
launched in London yesterday to raise cash to help pay for
former child migrants to return to find family.

The foundation, based in Perth, will seek contributions
from the Australian and British governments, churches and
charities.

More than 3000 children went sent to Australia between 1938 and 1963 under a joint scheme by the two
governments, with many of the youngsters from Catholic
institutions. The initiative is now widely condemned.

Often the children were not orphans, but were born out
of wedlock or from broken homes. Many parents now say
they were told their children had died or been adopted.

Controversy over the program was fuelled last year
when archives revealed some of the children were physically
and sexually abused.

Mary Gandy, general secretary of the Catholic Child
Welfare Council, which is working with the Australian Child
Migrant Foundation, said many of the migrants, now in their
late 50s and 60s, had traced relatives in Britain but were
unable to afford a visit.

"We want to raise money essential for fares for other
migrants," she said. "If we can achieve that we will be doing
something very valuable."

Ms Gandy said for many of the migrants, time was
running out. The council already knew of people who had
located their relatives in the UK only to discover they had
recently died.

Two brothers, Frank and Des Marshall, who helped launch the campaign, were recently reunited with sisters in Belfast after 40 years. A brother Paddy they never met died 18 months ago.

"I know a lot of people in Australia who would love to come back, even if it's just to a gravestone so they can feel they belong somewhere," said Frank, 51, a former hospital worker in Western Australia.

Frank and two brothers were sent to a children's home run by the Christian Brothers when he was 13, while his four sisters and another brother remained in Belfast with their father.

The Christian Brothers currently finances trips by about 15 ex-residents a year. The Brothers recently apologised over alleged sexual abuse of boys sent in its institution.

IN CONCLUSION, I feel that those who read this book will agree that the H.M.S. M.V. *Georgic* 'Super Trooper' was not such a bad ship and that troubles were caused by a minority of untrained, non-seafarers — and that this great ship should be left to rest in peace.

Stephen O'Hanlon
Author